GASTROPARESIS COOk

TABLE OF CONTENTS

Food is required for the proper functioning of the body, as it supplies nutrients that the body's cells use for energy, growth, and cell repair. However, before food can accomplish that, it must be adequately digested, meaning it must be broken down into tiny bits so that our bodies can absorb and utilize it. The digestive systems responsible for breaking down food materials into carbohydrates, protein, fats, and vitamins include the gastrointestinal tract, liver, pancreas, and gallbladder, etc.

A situation where the body's digestive system cannot digest the food consumed is known as gastroparesis. Human reports regarding physiology and anatomy state that immediately after you swallow any food, especially coarse food material, the stomach muscle walls begin to grind the consumed material into smaller particles. The grounded food particles are then transported into the small intestine and other stomach compartments.

However, when someone has gastroparesis, the stomach muscles stop functioning correctly. One of the apparent symptoms is that digestion will take longer because the small intestine will not empty its contents quickly. Thus, gastroparesis delays digestion, leading to other complications affecting the human body. Although the causes of gastroparesis are unknown, statistically, 9 out of 10 people with GP have diabetes mellitus, postoperative or idiopathic forms (spontaneous eruption of unknown cause).

HOW COMMON IS GASTROPARESIS?

It has been shown that gastroparesis affects less than 1% of the world population. A study carried out with 3604 gastroparesis patients identified that gastroparesis in males was 9.6 per 100,000 and 38 per 100,000 for women. In a European study, the prevalence of gastroparesis was calculated at 13.8 per 100,000 people, with a 1.9 per 100,000 person-year incidences. Also, research has shown that overall survival is worse in diabetic and gastroparesis patients. In a cross-sectional population-based investigation in the United States, gastroparesis was found in 4.6 percent of type 1 and 1.3 percent of type 2 diabetics.

WHO IS MORE LIKELY TO DEVELOP GASTROPARESIS?

It is important to note that certain people tend to develop gastroparesis due to some circumstances that they have found themselves in. However, this condition is generally more common in women than men, as only one out of five patients are male. Aside from gender, other factors may increase one's ability to develop gastroparesis, and they include:

- Diabetic patients

- People have undergone some forms of surgery in their stomach, especially on their small intestine. During this surgery, several damages are often caused to the vagus nerve, which controls the stomach and small intestine muscles.

- Cancer patients

People diagnosed with gastroparesis must continually visit the doctor to observe further complications, some of which may arise from fermented food in the stomach, which causes the growth of bacteria. Other times, undigested food can harden and form a bezoar mass, leading to nausea and vomiting. In addition, for diabetic patients, gastroparesis can make it challenging to manage their blood sugar levels and maintain a healthy weight.

CHAPTER ONE

WHAT IS GASTROPARESIS?

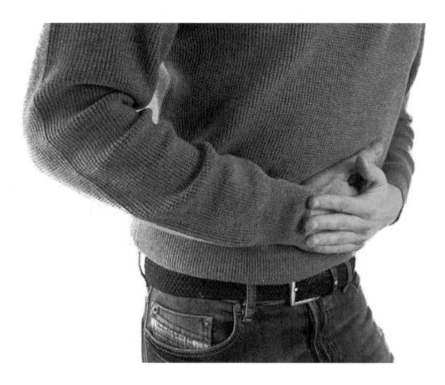

It is important to note that the stomach consists of a flexible sac that is elastic during digestion. As a result, the stomach empties its content into the small intestine. However, gastroparesis is a disease that reduces the stomach's ability to empty its contents. This is due to the absence or lack of peristaltic movements in the muscles of the patients suffering from gastroparesis. Thereby altering the involuntary contraction of stomach tissue, causing food to accumulate in the organ.

SYMPTOMS OF GASTROPARESIS

The frequent signs that allow us to identify this disease are:

- **Nausea and vomiting:** When vomiting occurs, food that has not undergone appreciable digestion is expelled. This is because the peristaltic movement of the food material is very slow and may cause irritation of the guts.

- **Lack of appetite:** The patient loses weight in a short time and begins to demonstrate specific nutritional deficits. Hypoglycemia may occur. Lack of appetite can lead to reduced fluids, which could lead to dehydration of the patient.

- **Abdominal inflammation** is accompanied by discomfort that varies in intensity over time. This is due to the excessive accumulation of food in the stomach. This symptom is also called bloating.

- **Easily Satisfied after eating a small amount of food:** Most people suffering from gastroparesis do not eat much because they are easily satisfied.

- **Abdominal pain or cramping:** This is another symptom of gastroparesis as the undigested food can lead to severe abdominal pains making the patient unable to move a long distance

- **Heartburn:** This symptom is common among women

- **Inconsistent blood sugar levels are** also common in diabetic patients.

CAUSES OF GASTROPARESIS

Currently, the causes of gastroparesis are unknown. However, according to clinical studies, it is believed that there is a relationship between damage to the vagus nerve and this disorder. In this way, this nerve causes the involuntary contractions that develop in this organ and push food into the small intestine. It is possible to point out medical conditions that cause injury and alter the functions of the vagus nerve are:

- Diabetes.

- Reduced activity is due to the thyroid gland (Hypothyroidism).

- Diseases of the Central Nervous System (CNS). For example, Parkinson's disease.

- Surgical interventions in the esophagus, stomach, or small intestine

- Certain drugs. For example, opioid medications or anticholinergics.

- An infection in the stomach tissue can also cause it.

Your health care provider will do a physical exam and ask about your health history. You may have specific tests and tests, such as:

- **Blood tests.** They allow checking the levels of different blood cells. They also measure the levels of chemicals and minerals (electrolytes).

- **Upper gastrointestinal series.** It is also known as an esophageal transit test or esophagography. This study reviews the esophagus and stomach. The first part of the small intestine (duodenum) is also seen. The study involves swallowing a liquid that can be seen on x-rays. The fluid in the stomach is then tracked with x-rays.

- **Gastric emptying scan.** This test allows the provider to see the food in the stomach during the study. In addition, you can see how quickly food leaves the stomach. Food labeled with a radioisotope is swallowed to be tracked with a scanner to determine how long it takes to reach the stomach.

  - **Breath test to measure gastric emptying.** This test measures how quickly a meal containing a specific non-radioactive form of carbon leaves the stomach. Carbon is absorbed in the top of the gastrointestinal tract. It is then exhaled in the breath.

  - **Gastric emptying of radiopaque markers.** This test allows us to see how quickly small plastic markers mixed with food come out of the stomach. Again, the features are seen on X-rays.

- **Gastric manometry.** It is also known as gastroduodenal manometry. This test evaluates muscle movement in the stomach and small intestine.

- **Upper endoscopy.** While you are sedated, the doctor uses an endoscope to look inside the esophagus, stomach, and duodenum. This test is essential to rule out that no other conditions besides gastroparesis cause your symptoms.

- **Wireless capsule endoscopy.** You need to swallow a small capsule with a small chamber inside for this test. This test measures the emptying of the stomach.

- **Gastric accommodation test by scintigraphy.** This test also uses foods labeled with a radioisotope tracked with a scanner to measure what's in the stomach before and after eating. This allows you to control how your stomach relaxes after eating food.

TREATMENT OF DIABETIC GASTROPARESIS

Your health care provider will design a care plan for you that may include:

- **The use of medicines.** Certain drugs will be given to you to help improve blood sugar levels, relieve nausea and vomiting, or act on your digestive system muscles. Your health care provider may prescribe several medicines to see which one works best.

- **Stop taking some medicines.** The health care provider may request an abrupt stopping of certain medications. This is because some of the medications may cause slow digestion.

- **Dietary Change.** Altering your eating habits to manage the situation.

- **Gastric neurotransmitter.** This device can help control nausea and vomiting. It is placed on the body through surgery. It helps stimulate the stomach muscles.

- **Intravenous feeding(parenteral nutrition).** This is for severe cases where a person cannot eat food by mouth. Instead, nutrients are introduced directly into the veins. For example, in surgery, a tube is inserted into one of the veins in your chest. A bag of liquid nutrients or medicine is attached to that tube several times a day.

- **Surgery.** When the case is very extreme, there may be some surgical operation. This surgery may include inserting a feeding tube into the small intestine through the abdomen. This tube allows nutrients to go directly to the small intestine instead of the stomach.

HOW TO CHANGE YOUR DIET

These changes can help reduce the problem:

- Make six small meals throughout the day instead of 3 large meals.

- Make a few liquid meals per day instead of solid. You may need to do this until your blood sugar levels stabilize.

- Do not eat foods with high-fat content. This includes fried foods, fatty meats, and dairy products with high-fat content. These foods can slow your digestion.

- Do not eat foods high in insoluble fiber. This includes beans and many vegetables and fruits. These can be difficult to digest.

POSSIBLE COMPLICATIONS OF DIABETIC GASTROPARESIS

When you consume some meal and stay within the small intestine, it may lead to certain complications. Food can ferment in the stomach. This causes the growth of bacteria. Undigested food can also harden and form a mass called a bezoar. This can lead to nausea and vomiting.

These complications may prevent food from passing from the stomach to the small intestine in some cases. The challenges may make it difficult for gastroparesis to manage their blood sugar levels. It can also cause problems for the body to absorb vitamins and minerals. It can make it challenging to maintain a healthy weight.

CHAPTER TWO

DAY 1: GETTING STARTED

After familiarizing yourself with the fundamental principles for a gastroparesis diet, it's time to consider what you're going to consume. The following pages include a list of meals that are GP-friendly. Consider it a jumping-off place for your experiments. This list is not exhaustive; indeed, some other foods and goods may be safely incorporated into a gastroparesis diet. Consider the nutrition data and ingredient list when determining if a GP-friendly product.

Pay close attention to each meal's fat and fiber content and look out for non-GP-friendly items, such as dried fruit, nuts, or seeds. Above all, take into account your personal tolerances and previous experiences. Choosing what to eat may first feel daunting, but it does become easier, and I encourage you to continue trying and broadening your nutritional options as much as possible. In addition, having a diverse selection of well-tolerated, GP-approved alternatives on hand can help alleviate the stress, boredom, and nutritional concerns that often accompany a restricted diet.

Breakfast is the most important food you can consume as a gastroparesis patient. Without eating breakfast, you may lose a lot of weight due to severe dietary concerns. Below is a list of food you can consume on the first day of your dietary plan as a gastroparesis patient.

CHESTNUT PANCAKES:

Chestnut pancakes are very easy to make and digest. One of the advantages of consuming chestnuts as gastroparesis is that they are low in fat and high in vitamin C. Chestnut flour has a sweet taste; for this reason, it is advisable not to abound with sugar or honey. In most cases, pancakes are usually accompanied by maple syrup, but, in this case, honey or hazelnut cream are valid alternatives.

Ingredients

- Chestnut flour: 5 oz.
- Egg: 4 oz
- Milk: 7 oz.
- Honey: 2 oz.
- Butter: 1.5 oz.
- Yeast for cakes: 0.1 oz.

Preparation

- In a bowl, beat the egg, add 1 oz of butter melted in a double boiler, honey, and milk.
- Proceed to put the sifted flour with the baking powder. Mix well, avoiding making lumps.
- Grease a non-stick pan with the remaining butter. As soon as it is hot, pour 2tsp of the mixture into the pan to distribute it evenly. As soon as bubbles have formed on the surface, turn the pan and cook for another minute. Continue until the dough is used up. Serve with honey.

Nutrition:

- Calories: 40g

- Carb: 150g

- Fat: 12g

- Fiber: 3g

- Protein: 9g

WHITE RICE WITH MOZZARELLA

White rice is a special kind of breakfast encouraged for gastroparesis patients. It is very easy to make, and the digestion time is relatively short. This meal is very nutritious and is filled with rustic flavors. White rice breaks down quickly in your digestive tract, and your body uses that sugar as an energy source.

Ingredients

- Rice: 13 oz.

- Frozen peas: 4 oz.

- Mozzarella: 5 oz.

- Oil: 3 tsp

- 2 cloves of Garlic: 1.3 oz.

- Salt: 0.5 oz.

- Pepper: 0.4 oz.

- Water: 5 cups

Preparation

- Put a clove of garlic with three tablespoons of oil in a non-stick pan, wait for it to brown and then add the rice first and then the hot water. Next, add the peas and close with the lid. Cook for 10-15 minutes, respecting the cooking instructions for the rice you used.

- It should be turned, and the water level checked if necessary.

- Season with salt and pepper when the rice is soft; add the diced mozzarella. Stir, and the mozzarella will melt with only the heat of the rice.

Nutrition:

- Calories: 180g

- Carb: 20g

- Fat: 7g

- Fiber: 0.4g

- Protein: 8g

ROASTED CHICKEN WITH ZUCCHINI

There are several benefits of eating this recipe in the morning, and one of them is that it is satisfying regardless of the quantity consumed. In addition, roasted chicken is very rich in protein and low in fat, which is essential for gastroparesis patients with diabetes.

Ingredients

- Chicken: 70 oz.

- One clove of Garlic: 0.5 oz.

- Salt: 0.4 oz.

- Pepper: 0.5 oz.

- Courgettes: 2 oz.

- Oregano: 0.5 oz.

- Zucchini: 32 oz.

Preparation

- Heat a non-stick pan till it gets very hot; add a little oil and cut the chicken into small pieces with all the skin. After 10 minutes, the skin will be brown.

- Lower the heat and add a clove of garlic while browning the chicken on all sides. It will be ready after 30-35 minutes of cooking; it must not be too dry inside. Add salt and pepper only for the last 10 minutes of cooking.

- Cut the courgettes into strips as noodles and sprinkle them with oil.

- Include salt with pepper, and lemon juice should be added.

- Add a little oregano and leave them to steep.

Nutrition:

- Calories: 250g

- Carb: 11g

- Fat: 2g

- Fiber: 3.8

- Protein: 45g

Due to the rapid filling of most gastroparesis patients, avoid meals and beverages that take up a lot of space without giving many nutrients, such as diet drinks, puffed or whipped foods, and so on. Rather than that, start with nutrient-dense meals that include a high concentration of vitamins, calories, and protein in a small volume, such as smooth nut butter, oils, fresh juices, and smoothies. The following is a list of foods that you may take during lunch:

WATERMELON AND CUCUMBER SALAD

The watermelon and cucumber salad is a tasty dish for lunch. This is a special kind of amino acid that aids blood movement in your body and lowers blood pressure. Also, cucumbers are very nutritious, although they are deficient in calories but high in vitamins and minerals.

Ingredients

- Watermelon: 18 oz.

- Cucumbers: 32 oz.

- Onions: 5 oz.

- Feta Cheese: 8 oz.

- Mint: 0.5 oz.

- Salt: 0.4 oz.

- Extra virgin olive oil: As required

Preparation

- Wash the cucumbers well and remove the ends; cut them into thin slices without peeling.

- Cut the watermelon into cubes about two centimeters thick.

- Obtain skinny slices from the onion.

- Arrange all the ingredients in a large salad bowl and add the crumbled feta together with a few well-washed mint leaves.

- Season with salt and a drizzle of extra virgin olive oil, then cover with cling film and leave to settle in the refrigerator for 10 minutes.

- Serve the salad as soon as it has been removed from the fridge.

Nutrition:

- Calories: 219g

- Carb: 15g

- Fat: 5.6g

- Fiber: 1.2g

- Protein: 5.3g

PASTA WITH BAKED TOMATOES

The pasta with tomatoes in the oven is a simple but tasty dish easily digested. Making the sauce for this pasta does not require any complicated steps; indeed, it is a perfect recipe even for the less accustomed in the kitchen: just put the whole tomatoes in the oven and let them cook. The cooked tomatoes contain high levels of antioxidants, and the pasta contains a good energy source.

Ingredient:

- Pasta: 12 oz.

- Tomatoes: 17 oz.

- Mozzarella: 12 oz.

- Basil: As required

- Oregano: As required

- 2 cloves of Garlic: 1 oz.

- Salt: As required

- Extra virgin olive oil: As required

Preparation

- For the first step, dedicate yourself to the sauce: take an oven dish, wash the tomatoes thoroughly and arrange them all whole in the pan; peel the garlic cloves and add them to the tomatoes, season with a pinch of salt, a drizzle of extra virgin olive oil and a pinch of oregano.

- Next, put everything in a hot oven at 200 ° C for about 20 minutes without ever touching them until they are soft and with a light crust.

- Meanwhile, cook the pasta in plenty of boiling salted water and drain.

- Take the tomatoes from the oven, remove the garlic cloves, and pour half the tomatoes into a big empty basin

- The next step is to pound with a fork and add the pasta and the remaining tomatoes with seasoning.

- You will need to cut a few fresh basil leaves and add the mozzarella cut into small pieces and drain from its water; mix everything with a wooden spoon, leave to settle for 10 minutes, and serve.

- Pasta with baked tomatoes is excellent, both warm and cold.

Nutrition:

- Calories: 300g

- Carb: 66.8g

- Fat: 3.2g

- Fiber: 1.2g

- Protein: 5.1g

Pasta with cold tuna is a complete dish to prepare in advance and enjoy on warm summer days. This recipe has been shown to contain a high level of omega-3 fatty acids, which helps to reduce heart disease. Aside from the nutritional benefits, it can be digested easily, slow the growth of tumor cells, and reduce body inflammation.

Ingredients

- Pasta: 10 oz.

- Tomatoes: 8.8 oz.

- Tuna: 7 oz.

- Black olives: 3.5 oz.

- Basil as required

- Extra virgin olive oil: As required

- Salt: As required

Preparation

- Put the pasta in abundant salted boiling water, drain it once.

- The next step is to place it inside a glass container and immerse it in ice water to stop cooking. Next, put extra virgin olive oil and mix so that the pasta does not stick and let it cool.

- Carefully wash the cherry tomatoes and cut them in half, put them in a large container together with the whole olives, and the tuna fillets drained completely from the preserving oil.

- Pour the pasta into the sauce, season with salt, and chop a few basil leaves by hand. Use a spatula to homogenize the mixture and rest in the refrigerator for 30 minutes before serving.

Nutrition:

- Calories: 292g

- Carb: 58g

- Fat: 1.3g

- Fiber: 2.2g

- Protein: 26.3g

You have to realize that the quantity of fiber tolerated varies per patient, although a normal gastroparesis diet should include around 10-15 grams of fiber per day. Additionally, patients are advised to avoid high-fiber meals such as fresh fruits and vegetables and whole grains. Rather than that, choose lower-fiber alternatives such as well-cooked meat or juiced vegetables, cooked or pureed fruits, white rice, maize or rice cereals, and sourdough or French bread for dinner.

PEPPER ROAST PORK

The pig roast pepper is another tasty dish, perfect for a meat menu and easy to accomplish. However, it is not a dish for everyone, especially those who do not like spicy cuisine. On the contrary, however, it is the perfect dish for adding pepper to any dish. The pepper roast pork recipe can be flavored with black, pink, or green peppers. Each type, inevitably, gives a different aftertaste and degree of spiciness, so it is good to choose according to your preferences. As for the cut of meat, you can select the fillet or the pork loin, in addition to the loin. Accompany it with baked potatoes, and you will have brought a perfectly balanced second course to the table.

Ingredients

- Pork loin: 25 oz.

- Extra virgin olive oil: 4 tbsp

- Garlic powder: 2 tsp

- Pepper: As required

- Red chili powder: ½ tsp

- Dry chopped bay leaf: 1 tsp

- Paprika: 1 tsp

- Salt: As required

Preparation

- You will need to heat the oven to 175 ° C. Place the loin on a baking sheet. Collect the olive oil, garlic, paprika, black pepper, red pepper, bay leaf, salt, and pepper in a bowl.

- Stir and rub the mixture over the pork loin so that it is completely covered with it.

- Drizzle with plenty of oil and transfer to the oven. Cook for 35-45 minutes.

- If you have a cooking thermometer, you must wait for it to reach a temperature of 69 ° C inside.

- Bring it from the oven, let it rest for 5 minutes, then slice and serve.

Nutrition:

- Calories: 205.1g

- Carb: 2.2g

- Fat: 1.3g

- Fiber: 0.4g

- Protein: 31.9g

Baked chicken is a spectacular dish to have on the table for dinner. One of the significant reasons chicken is advised as dinner is that it is a slice of lean meat with high nutritional value. Another advantage is that eating it regularly will help you stay healthy. It is essential to note that you can use potatoes as a side dish, while for the aromas, you can choose thyme, marjoram, bay leaf, sage, or even chili if you love spicy.

Ingredients

- Chicken: 55 oz.

- Rosemary oil: 4 tbsp

- Potatoes: 22 oz.

- 4 cloves of Garlic: 1.2 oz.

- Salt: As needed

- Extra virgin olive oil: As required

Preparation

- Take a sprig of rosemary and finely chop the needles; in the same way, chop the garlic and put both in a small bowl with plenty of extra virgin olive oil. Add some salt and mix. Leave aside.

- Take the chicken and arrange it in a relatively large pan. Tie the thighs with kitchen string and insert a clove of unpeeled garlic and a sprig of the whole rosemary inside the animal.

- Take the rosemary oil and pour it all over the outside of the chicken, massaging it with your fingers so that the aromas and salt absorb it well.

- Place the pan with the chicken in a preheated oven at 200 ° C and cook for an hour, wetting the chicken from time to time with the sauce that is being formed.

- Meanwhile, wash and peel the potatoes. Cut them into rather large wedges and put them to soak in cold water. Drain them, put them in a bowl, and season with salt, a little extra virgin olive oil, and the remaining rosemary.

- After the chicken's cooking time, take out the pan and surround the chicken with the potatoes. Put the remaining garlic cloves and cook for another 30 minutes.

- When the chicken is golden brown and the potatoes soft, it's ready.

Nutrition:

- Calories: 187g

- Carb: 1.3g

- Fat: 0.3g

- Fiber: 0g

- Protein: 30g

STEW WITH SAUCE

The stew with sauce is a classic meal for family lunch and dinner. Veal is made very tender by slow cooking, and the sauce is also suitable for seasoning pasta, thus having a rich and tasty single dish. This meal is preferable because it mixes several nutrients and its filling ability.

Ingredients

- Veal: 18 oz.

- Tomato sauce: 16 oz.

- Onions: As required

- Bay leaf: 4 oz.

- Extra virgin olive oil: As required

- Salt: As required

Preparation

- Cut the onion into a small bit and brown it in a large pot with extra virgin olive oil drizzle. Add the meat cut into regular pieces and brown it on all sides over high heat.

- Add the bay leaves to a saucepan and season with salt. If needed, add a glass of hot water to cover the meat.

- Cover with the lid and let the stew cook over low heat for about 45 minutes, stirring occasionally.

- Once the sauce is creamy and the meat tender, turn off the heat and let it rest for a few minutes before serving.

- Bring the stew to the table and enjoy with a loaf of good homemade bread.

Nutrition:

- Calories: 318g

- Carb: 13g

- Fat: 15g

- Fiber: 1.1g

- Protein: 35g

WHAT CONSTITUTES A "MINI-MEAL?"

When you consume tiny meals throughout the day, it's easy to get into a snacking mentality, preferring single items such as crackers, yogurt, or bananas over well-balanced meals. While this is the simplest option, it is neither the healthiest nor most satisfying. Mini-meals should be as balanced as possible, with tiny servings of easily digestible carbs, protein, and a little amount of fat. For instance:

Breakfast: 1 cup heated cereal 1/2 banana or 4 oz pureed fruit

Lunch: 1 cup chicken noodle soup 1 tbsp butter on a little white bun

Dinner: 2 oz. skinless roasted chicken breast 1/2 cup mashed potatoes 1/2 cup vegetable puree

Additionally, nutritional supplement beverages and some smoothies provide balanced snacks between breakfast, lunch, and supper.

HOW CAN I STOP LOSING WEIGHT?

Many people with gastroparesis first lose weight due to acute symptoms or dietary restrictions. To minimize more weight loss, concentrate on optimizing the nutrients in each bite or drink. For example, avoid meals and beverages that take up a lot of space without giving many nutrients, e.g., soft drinks and fat-free cookies. Instead, eat nutrient-dense meals high in vitamins, calories, and healthy fats, such as smooth nut butter, oils, fresh juices, and smoothies.

WHY AM I GAINING WEIGHT WITH GP?

While many gastroparesis patients have difficulty losing weight, others effortlessly maintain or increase weight while eating very little. This may be a direct result of poor dieting, a high carbohydrate diet, continuous snacking, or underlying issues. Notably, metabolic diseases such as hypothyroidism may result in delayed stomach emptying and weight gain. Therefore, consider monitoring your thyroid if you continue to gain weight after being diagnosed with idiopathic gastroparesis.

Unfortunately, many physicians disregard the problems of obese GP patients. Regardless of your weight, it is important to locate a physician who will take you and your problems seriously. To prevent more weight gain, concentrate on well-balanced mini-meals, include some fat into your diet to satisfy both your mind and body and incorporate moderate activity into your daily routine.

CHAPTER THREE

DAY 2: EATING WITH CARE

Continuously check the fiber content of packaged foods, even if you've purchased the product before. More and more food manufacturers are adding inulin or digestion-resistant maltodextrin to boost fiber content. Unfortunately, this added fiber can turn an otherwise GP-friendly product into just the opposite. For example, some fat-free creamy vanilla ice cream now contains 3 grams of fiber per half-cup serving. So, if you eat one cup of the ice cream, you'll consume about half of the daily total recommended fiber intake for gastroparesis patients.

WHOLE FOODS VS. OVER PROCESSED FOODS

Processed foods, in general, are devoid of nutrients and dense in artificial additives. Also, some chemicals prevalent in traditional packaged foods, such as high fructose corn syrup and sugar alcohols, may lead to bloating, distention, and bowel irregularity in certain people.

BREAKFAST

When adhering to a gastroparesis diet, it's all too easy to get used to eating the same things over and over again. Meals with family or friends may be challenging to prepare and consume. I've included a range of recipes in this area in the hopes that they may improve the pleasure and nutritious quality of your diet, as well as assist you in regaining some feeling of "normalcy." All of the recipes are deemed "GP-Friendly" in general. Again, it's important to remember that not every recipe will suit every gastroparesis sufferer. Small adjustments to the ingredients to produce a meal that is specially tailored to your dietary restrictions. For day two, here are some excellent recipe options:

RICE NOODLES WITH SHRIMP

Rice noodles with shrimp is a tasty dish of Chinese cuisine that requires very fast and simple preparation. However, like many recipes highlighted in this book, it is very easy to digest and tasty. This meal gives the gastroparesis patient something extraordinary from their usual course meal.

Ingredients

- Rice noodles pasta: 11 oz.

- Shrimps (tails): 8 oz.

- Coral beans: 5 oz.

- Asparagus: 3.5 oz.

- Spring onions: As required

- Extra virgin olive oil: As required

- Salt: As required

Preparation

- Clean the snow peas and asparagus, cut them evenly, and cook them in a cooking pan where you have softened the finely sliced onion with a drizzle of oil.

- Add the shrimp tails and continue to cook for about 5 minutes over medium heat.

- Proceed to add the soy sauce.

- Meanwhile, boil the rice noodles for 3-4 minutes, separating them with the help of a fork. Then, remove the water from the noodles and pour them into the wok together with the other ingredients.

Nutrition:

- Calories: 240g

- Carb: 34g

- Fat: 3.5g

- Fiber: 4.8g

- Protein: 17g

BAKED NOODLES WITH PEAS AND HAM

The noodle bake is a prime dish for breakfast. It is easy to prepare and practical because it can be cooked in advance and kept in the refrigerator until baking. In addition, these foods help digestive health and fuel healthy gut microbes. This diet is also suitable for patients with type 2 diabetes because it maintains the balance of the body systems.

Ingredients

- Pasta (noodles): 15 oz.

- Flour: 2 oz.

- Butter: 2.5 oz.

- Diced cooked ham: 5.4 oz.

- Onions: As required

- Carrots: As required

- Bechamel: 4 tbsp

- Salt: As required

- Pepper: As required

- Rosemary oil: As required

- Peas: 7 oz.

- Parmesan: 5 oz.

- Extra virgin olive oil: 3 tbsp

Preparation

- Finely chop the onion, celery, and carrot. Fry the mirepoix thus obtained in 2 tablespoons of oil until the vegetables are soft.

- Add the peas and continue cooking until soft. Add the cooked ham and season with salt and pepper. Add a few needles of rosemary.

- Season the pasta with the béchamel and the peas with the ham. Also, add the Parmesan. Grease the single-portion casseroles with the remaining spoonful of oil, sprinkle with breadcrumbs, and arrange the pasta. Bake it for about fifteen minutes; activate the grill function for 5 minutes to brown the surface. Serve hot.

Nutrition:

- Calories: 390g

- Carb: 96g

- Fat: 8g

- Fiber: 13g

- Protein: 29g

An omelet with smoked salmon and green onions is a hearty and delicious breakfast. This breakfast is simple to digest and quick to prepare if you're in a rush.

Ingredients

- Two Eggs: 4 oz.

- Salmon smoked: 1.5 oz.

- Butter: 1 tsp

- A clove of garlic: 0.5 oz.

- Herbs: As required

- Salt: As required

Preparation

- Rinse the onion and carefully slice it.

- Lightly beat eggs with spices, garlic, and herbs.

- Thinly slice the fish, then cut it into tiny strips or cubes.

- Homogenize the butter and eggs. Stir with a spatula, then gather the eggs from end to center and fry them.

- Add the garlic, smoked salmon, and green onions when the egg mass has curdled. Simmer the scrambled eggs for a few minutes more to allow them to set and cook properly. You may control the degree to which eggs are fried.

- Always serve the omelet with smoked salmon hot, with toast. It is important to try this recipe for breakfast to have energy for the rest of the day.

Nutrition:

- Calories: 200

- Fat: 10g

- Fiber: 2g

- Carbs: 11g

- Protein: 15g

Taking a lunch break is not always possible, but it is necessary for gastroparesis patients' health and sanity on many occasions. Lunch gives the body and brain the energy and nutrition they need to function correctly during the afternoon. According to experts, eating lunch offers nutrients to the body and brain while reducing stress. According to the researchers, eating lunch also provides a recess from the day's activities while also providing energy for the remainder of the afternoon. Here are some of the lunches that you can consume on your day two:

MUFFINS WITH BACON AND CHEDDAR CHEESE

Ingredients

- Bacon: 10 oz.

- Cauliflower: 1.5 oz.

- Cabbage: 2 oz.

- Baking powder: 1 tsp

- Almond flour: 3.5 oz.

- Three eggs: 9 oz.

- Pepper: As required

- Onions: As required

- Ground Garlic: 1.5 oz.

- Salt: As required

- Cheddar cheese: 2 oz.

Preparation

- Fry the bacon and transfer it to a paper towel. Ensure it cools down slightly and cut it.

- Grind the cauliflower in a blender consistently and transfer it to a bowl. Add the remainder of the ingredients, bacon, and stir thoroughly. Leave some cheese for sprinkling.

- Arrange the dough in pans, sprinkle with grated cheese on top, and bake in an oven set to 170 ° C for 25-30 minutes until golden brown.

Nutrition:

- Calories: 235g

- Carb: 144g

- Fat: 13g

- Fiber: 5g

- Protein: 30g

ZUCCHINI WAFFLES WITH PARMESAN

Ingredients

- Zucchini: 30 oz.

- Two eggs: 5 oz.

- Almond Paste: 2.8 oz.

- Grated Parmesan Cheese: 2.1 oz.

- Salt: As required

- Pepper: As required

- Two cloves of Garlic: 1 oz.

Preparation

- With a cheesecloth or paper towel, wring out the zucchini's excess water and rub it. Add the rest of the ingredients to the zucchini and combine thoroughly.

- Place the dough in a hot waffle iron and cook for 7-9 minutes to make waffles. Finally, remove the waffles from the waffle iron and allow them to cool before serving.

Nutrition:

- Calories: 261g

- Carb: 6g

- Fat: 15g

- Fiber: 2g

- Protein: 17g

Ingredients

- Butter: 2 tsp

- Almond flour: 2 tsp

- Salt: As required

- Cream: 4 oz.

- Grated cheese: 4 oz.

- Chopped green onions: 1 tsp

- Four eggs: 12 oz.

Preparation

- Lightly oil the four molds and sprinkle with almond flour inside.

- Ensure that you divide the four eggs into each mold.

- Melt the butter in a skillet, add almond flour, salt, and fry, occasionally stirring for 2 minutes

- Reduce the heat and put a little amount of cream

- Cook for five minutes, stirring occasionally. Add cheese, onion, and stir.

- Add yolks to the mixture and stir.

- Separate the egg whites with a mixer until firm peaks.

- Gently insert proteins into the base

- Pour the dough into four tins and place in an oven preheated to 180 ° C for 20 minutes.

Nutrition:

- Calories: 404g

- Carb: 23g

- Fat: 14g

- Fiber: 0.4g

- Protein: 16g

Dinner is a critical meal, and you may experiment with a wide variety of delicious items. Good sleep, healthier breakfast and lunch choices, reduced inflammation, higher resistance to stress, improved digestion, stable blood sugar, and decreased anxiety are all connected to a nutritious supper.

DANISH CHEESE PUFF

Ingredients

- Mozzarella cheese: 7 oz.

- Cream cheese: 8 oz.

- Almond flour: 3 oz.

- Coconut flour: 0.7 oz.

- Baking powder: 2 tsp

- Two eggs: 5 oz.

- Erythritol: 2.5 oz.

- Salt: As requires

- Lemon juice: 1 tsp

- Butter: 1 tsp

- Cream: 0.5 oz.

Preparation

- Combine cream cheese, erythritol, lemon juice, and egg yolk.

- The dough should be enriched with mozzarella and cream cheese. When the cheese is melted, microwave it (heat for a minute, and stir for 30 seconds until it becomes soft and homogeneous).

- Using 0.5 oz. of erythritol in addition to the baking powder, egg, and almond/coconut flours, you may create a well-balanced batter.

- After splitting the dough in half, it should be rolled out to a thickness of about 5 mm. Divide the area into four sections of the same size. Make a notch in each of the corner's four sides. When it's finished, fold in all four corners with a spoonful of the topping in the middle.

- Put it inside the oven and bake at 180 degrees Celsius for 12-15 minutes.

- While baking, combine erythritol powder, butter, cream cheese, and a little salt in a small saucepan. Melt on medium heat until smooth. When the pastry bag is used to drizzle the frosting onto the puffs, they are done.

Nutrition:

- Calories: 263g

- Carb: 43g

- Fat: 18g

- Fiber: 2.9g

- Protein: 11.6g

Ingredients

- Tofu cheese: 13 oz.

- Turmeric: 2 oz.

- Yeast: 1 tsp

- Unsweetened almond milk: 6 oz.

- Salt: As required

- Pepper: As required

- Chopped Onions: 0.4 oz.

Preparation

- Break the tofu into tiny pieces in a non-stick pan.

- Add turmeric, yeast, and heat for 5 minutes.

- Add almond milk and boil for 10 minutes. Ensure that you often stir until the tofu is a little creamier.

Nutrition:

- Calories: 153g

- Carb: 23g

- Fat: 17g

- Fiber: 5g

- Protein: 35g

SANDWICH

Ingredients

- Five Egg: 15 oz.

- Cream: 4.2 oz.

- Erythritol: 1 tsp

- Almond flour: 2.5 tsp

- Baking Powder: ½ tsp

- Salt: As required

- Butter: 3 tsp

- Cutlets: 2 tsp

- Bacon Slice: 5 oz.

- Cheddar cheese: 2 oz.

Preparation

- Knock two eggs, cream cheese, and erythritol until frothy in a large bowl using an electric mixer. Mix both the almond flour, baking powder, and salt in a large bowl.

- Turn on the fire source and put the skillet on it. Pour a tablespoon of oil and fry four pancakes with melted butter. You will then fry for 1 to 2 minutes until the edges raise and quickly flip. Tenderize by frying for a further 2-3 minutes. While the burgers, bacon, and eggs are cooking, keep them warm.

- Cook the patties and bacon. Softly whisk three eggs in a hot pan, then cook half of them. To assemble, start with a pancake, then add the completed cutlet, followed by the egg, bacon, and cheese, before finishing with another pancake.

Nutrition:

- Calories: 525g

- Carb: 60g

- Fat: 18g

- Fiber: 2g

- Protein: 25g

WHAT COOKING EQUIPMENT IS BEST FOR GASTROPARESIS PATIENTS?

Purchasing the proper food ingredient and the right tools will make cooking and preparing gastroparesis-friendly meals easier. I recommend investing in the following:

- An immersion blender (for soups and purees)

- Blender or Magic Bullet (for smoothies)

- Potato ricer (for non-pasty mashed potatoes and other

- purees)

- Freezer or safe containers

- A good set of measuring cups (for portion control)

- Electric juicer (for fresh fruit and vegetable juices)

Depending on your tolerances, I also recommend keeping the following ingredients on hand, as they're used in several GP-friendly recipes:

- Non-fat cooking spray

- Eggs, egg whites, or Egg Beaters

- Milk or dairy products

- Low-fiber pasta

- White rice

- Almond or peanut butter

IS IT POSSIBLE TO EAT AT RESTAURANTS?

Going out to eat is possible for gastroparesis patients, though proper planning is helpful. Here are some tips:

1. Know what you're going to order before you arrive.

It can be uncomfortable to search a menu for GP-friendly items while others look on, asking whether or not there's anything you can eat. However, almost all chain restaurants are good news, and many independent establishments now post their menus online. Some also provide nutrition information, which is extremely valuable since seemingly healthy dishes can sometimes be loaded with fat.

2. Ask for what you want.

Order what you want, whether that means just a side dish or something on the children's menu.

3. Enjoy the company.

Maintain a thorough focus on people you're with and the conversation taking place rather than the food. While that's certainly easier said than done, being social and continuing to spend time with friends – even if that means watching other people eat food that you wish you could be eating – is usually better for the spirit than sitting at home alone

---

IS IT POSSIBLE TO MAINTAIN A HEALTHY VEGETARIAN DIET?

Gastroparesis patients can safely follow a vegetarian diet with extra planning and diligence. Choices would include:

- Fruits and vegetables

- Low-fiber grains

- Non-dairy milk

- Non-animal protein sources, such as nut butter, protein powders, and soy products

CHAPTER FOUR

DAY 3: BEWARE OF ADDED FIBER

Gastroparesis patients should eat a small number of meals frequently, and they should be low in fat and simple to digest so that you may obtain the nourishment you need. Eggs and creamy nut butter are two of the most diets to consume as a gastroparesis patient since they are strong in protein and simple to digest. Also, these meals are very easy to chew, swallow, and digest.

Dietary fiber is a group of compounds that the gastrointestinal tract cannot digest. Thus, colonic bacteria act on the consumed fiber through a fermentation process, causing a problem for gastroparesis patients. While fiber may have some advantages or benefits, it poses a great danger when consumed carelessly. Therefore, it is necessary to control and moderate the amount we eat.

Fiber does not allow glucose to pass quickly into the bloodstream and reduces the absorption of lipids. In addition, the intake of dietary fiber can decrease the absorption of essential minerals for the body, such as calcium, iron, zinc, and copper. Also, fiber intake does not have notable effects on vitamin absorption. Still, in vegetarian diets, the reduction in the availability of minerals such as iron and calcium, for example, and the low intake of food sources of the same, the risk of suffering deficiencies is superior.

In addition, another of the adverse effects of fiber intake is lower digestibility. This contributes to losing weight by providing more satiety and delaying gastric emptying, causing abdominal distention. Fiber has even been proven to reduce and inhibit the activity of pancreatic enzymes, which can alter the normal digestion of proteins, fats, and hydrates. For this reason, digestive problems can arise, and the availability of nutrients can be affected. However, all these negative effects of fiber intake can be reduced and avoided by simply controlling the amount consumed and not exceeding 30 grams per day.

BREAKFAST

A nutritious breakfast may increase memory, focus, creativity, problem-solving, and happiness. However, this section also explains the best breakfast you can eat on day 3 for healthy wellbeing.

PIZZA WITH PEPPERONI

Ingredients

- Almond flour: 4.3 oz.

- Coconut flour: 1.5 oz.

- Salt: As required

- Xanthan gum: 1 tsp

- Apple vinegar: 1 tsp

- Butter: 6 tsp

- Seven Egg: 15 oz.

- Mozzarella cheese: 3.5 oz.

- Pepperoni slice: 13 oz.

- Cream: 7.5 oz.

- Italian herbs: As required

Preparation

- Mix the almond flour, coconut flour, salt, xanthan gum, and vinegar inside the food processor.

- Continue pounding the dough until it resembles breadcrumbs.

- Then, add the egg and pulse once more.

- You will observe that the dough will form a ball. Wrap the dough in plastic wrap and refrigerate for 45-60 minutes.

- Use butter to rub the baking dish, pour the dough into it, and knead the bottom and edges with your fingers.

- On the base, arrange half of the cheese and pepperoni. Combine the eggs, cream, Provencal herbs, and salt in a mixing bowl. Fill a mold halfway with the mixture and top with the remaining cheese and pepperoni. Cover with foil and bake for about 35-45 minutes at 180 ° C. Remove the foil and bake for a further 10-15 minutes.

Nutrition:

- Calories: 416g

- Carb: 70g

- Fat: 38g

- Fiber: 3g

- Protein: 14g

Ingredient:

- Olive oil: 2 tsp

- Tomato: As required

- Onion powder: 2 tsp

- Garlic powder: 1 tsp

- Pepper: As required

- Salt: As required

- Cabbage: 3.5 oz.

- Two eggs: 4 oz.

Preparation

- Heat oil in a small cast-iron skillet, add chopped tomato and spices, fry for 3-4 minutes until soft.

- Cut and cook the cabbage for another 2-3 minutes. Make two compartments in the mixture and beat in the eggs

- Cover and cook for 4-5 minutes over low heat until the proteins have stabilized. Salt and serve.

Nutrition:

- Calories: 451g

- Carb: 90g

- Fat: 37g

- Fiber: 4g

- Protein: 15.6g

MCMUFFIN

Ingredients

- Four Egg: 10 oz.

- Grated Parmesan cheese: 1.1 oz.

- Cream cheese: 3.5 oz.

- Salt: As required

- Spices: As required

- Minced meat: 5.3 oz.

- Burger cheese: 2 oz.

Preparation

- Mix two yolks with Parmesan cheese, cream cheese, and a pinch of salt in a mixer.

- The mixer must mix the various elements together until it is smooth. Set away for later.

- Break about two eggs and gently mix the yolks and egg white into the mixture.

- Preheat a skillet over medium heat, add ¼ dough, and cook for about 2 minutes on each side.

- Form 2 cutlets from minced meat and fry in a pan until tender (about 4 minutes on each side). You will need to add the sliced cheese on top, with a tablespoon of water, into the pan and hold it for a minute under the lid.

- Place a round pan in a cold skillet, break an egg into it, and turn on and off medium heat. When the protein from the bottom grasps, stir the yolk, cover, and fry until tender.

Nutrition:

- Calories: 538g

- Carb: 30g

- Fat: 41g

- Fiber: 2g

- Protein: 37g

PANCAKES

Ingredients

- Almond flour: 3.17 oz.

- Coconut flour: 1.5 oz.

- Erythritol: 3 tsp

- Baking powder: 1 tsp

- Five eggs: 12 oz.

- Milk: 2.7 oz.

- Olive oil: 1.35 oz.

- Vanilla extract: 1 tsp

- Salt: As required

Preparation

- Combine the several ingredients in a bowl and mix them together until it is smooth. The dough should be the same consistency as a regular pancake dough. Do not add too much, or the pancakes will be too wet.

- Heat a greased skillet on the stove over medium heat. Pour the dough into the skillet and form into circles. Wait for about 2 minutes until bubbles begin to form. Turn over and cook for another 1.5-2 minutes, until browned on the other side.

Nutrition:

- Calories: 134g

- Carb: 3g

- Fat: 11.5g

- Fiber: 1.5g

- Protein: 45g

HOMEMADE CUPCAKE

Ingredients

- Vanilla Flavored: 1.5 oz.

- Almond flour: 1 cup

- Five Eggs: 14 oz.

- Butter: ½ cup

- Erythritol: 1 cup

- Baking powder: 2 tsp

- A pinch of salt

- Milk: ½ cup

Preparation

- Ensure that you melt the butter in the microwave.

- The next step is to mix the butter with the eggs, milk, baking powder, and salt using a mixer

- Furthermore, you are to add protein, flour, and erythritol and stir until smooth

- Bake in an oven for 32-37 minutes

Nutrition:

- Calories: 187g

- Carb: 23g

- Fat: 14g

- Fiber: 1g

- Protein: 14g

CHICKEN CUTLETS WITH CHEESE

Ingredients

- Chicken breast fillet: 26.5 oz.

- Two Eggs: 6 oz.

- Almond flour: 1.5 oz.

- Grated Cheddar cheese: 3.5 oz.

- Grated Parmesan cheese: 1.8 oz.

- Chopped green onions: 0.5 oz.

- Garlic powder: 1 tsp

- Salt as required

- Pepper as required

- Mayonnaise: 1 cup

- A clove of Garlic: 1 oz.

- Lemon juice: 1 tsp

Preparation

- In a food processor or mincer, cut up the chicken breasts

- Add salt and pepper to improve the taste. In addition, add garlic powder and the remaining ingredients to a large bowl and whisk until completely homogenizes. Set the mixed ingredients aside for 15 minutes.

- Mix mayonnaise with lemon juice and sliced garlic and chill for 15-30 minutes while the minced meat is infusing.

- Introduce a heat source to the skillet and add oil to cover the entire bottom of the skillet. Fry four patties at a time; broil until the top grasps, then flip and grill until tender. On average, 5-7 minutes on one side and 3-5 minutes on the other.

Nutrition:

- Calories: 160g

- Carb: 20g

- Fat: 9g

- Fiber: 1g

- Protein: 18g

SALMON CUTLETS

Ingredients

- Canned salmon: 5.3 oz.

- One egg: 3 oz.

- Mayonnaise: 2 tsp

- A clove of garlic: 0.5 oz.

- Ginger powder: 2 tsp

- Olive oil: 2 tsp

- Salt: As required

- Avocado: 3 oz.

- Sour cream: 1 cup

- Cilantro: 2 oz.

- Water: 2 cups

- Lemon juice: 2 tsp

Preparation

- Empty the salmon jar inside a bowl

- The next step is to combine both the fish, egg, mayonnaise, chopped garlic, ginger, and salt.

- Furthermore, you are to fry in olive oil for 4-5 minutes and ensure that it appears golden brown in color.

- For the sauce, combine the avocado pulp, sour cream, cilantro, tablespoon olive oil, and lemon juice in a blender. Add water until desired consistency is obtained.

Nutrition:

- Calories: 566g

- Carb: 50g

- Fat: 16g

- Fiber: 6g

- Protein: 20g

PORK FRIED RICE RECIPE

Chauhan is Japanese fried rice cooked with various ingredients: meat, vegetables, eggs, etc. It is a typical dish and an ideal way to use leftover rice in Japan. The ingredients vary greatly, and you can add whatever you have on hand.

Ingredients

- Cauliflower: 2 oz.

- Two eggs: 4 oz.

- Two cloves of garlic: 1 oz.

- Pork belly: 3.5 oz.

- Green mini peppers: 2 oz.

- Green onions: 2 oz.

- Soy sauce: 1 tsp

- Black sesame: 1 tsp

- Pickled ginger: 1 tsp

Preparation

- Gently slice the cauliflower and put it in the food processor. Heat some oil in a skillet, add cauliflower and sauté over medium heat for about 5 minutes. Remove from skillet and set aside

- Beat the eggs lightly and make a thin omelet. Remove from skillet and set aside

- Add the garlic to the skillet and, once flavorful, add the pork belly. While it's cooking, cut the omelet into small cubes.

- Add pepper to the cooked pork. Also, add green onions, and cook for another minute. Then add cauliflower and omelet

Nutrition:

- Calories: 400g

- Carb: 12g

- Fat: 12g

- Fiber: 4g

- Protein: 16g

Ingredients

- Chicken fillet: 5.3 oz.

- Avocado: 2 oz.

- Six boiled eggs: 18 oz.

- Sliced Bacon: 8 oz.

- Yogurt: 2 tsp

- Mayonnaise: 2 tsp

- Lemon juice: 2 tsp

- Freshly chopped cilantro: 0.7 oz.

- Salt as required

- Pepper as required

Preparation

- Dice the chicken, avocado, eggs, place them in a bowl, add yogurt, mayonnaise, lemon juice, and cilantro. Add extra salt, pepper and mix thoroughly

- Fry the bacon until crisp. Slice it into a tiny bit and sprinkle it on the salad.

Nutrition:

- Calories: 386g

- Carb: 45g

- Fat: 8g

- Fiber: 4g

- Protein: 23g

CAN ULTRA-PROCESSED FOOD BE CONSUMED REGULARLY?

Over the last several decades, the food business has penetrated our homes to make meal preparation simpler. Of course, the lack of time is the major reason why we turn to this kind of food, but what does the excess of ultra-processed signify in our health?

HOW ARE FOODS CLASSIFIED?

Unprocessed foods: These include natural fruits, vegetables, milk, meat, legumes, seeds, cereals, eggs.

Processed foods: These categories of food materials have been modified to have a long shelf life, better taste due to the addition of salt, oil, sugar, or fermentative materials. They include yogurts, cheese, ham, homemade bread, canned fruits, vegetables and legumes, smoked or canned fish, beer, and wine.

Ultra-processed foods: These categories of food material have been industrially processed synthetically or from compounds derived from other foods and sometimes have lengthy ingredient lists, including preservatives, sweeteners, or color and taste enhancers. This category includes processed meats like sausages and burgers, morning cereals and cereal bars, sauces, etc.

HOW DOES CONSUMPTION OF ULTRA-PROCESSED FOODS AFFECT HEALTH?

Most of these products have in their composition several of the following characteristics:

Small Nutrient: They are usually low in calories, with little nutrients.

Hydrogenated or trans fats: Fats generated by the food industry to make the product cheaper and more delicious.

Sugar: these products usually carry added sugar, which is not only present in pastries but also found in sauces, meat products, etc.

Salt: Salt makes the product last longer, as well as make it more hyper-palatable (A hyper-palatable food is one in which the synergy between the components of the food, such as fat, sodium (salt), sugar, and carbohydrates, makes it tastier than it would be)

Refined flours and oils: These have undergone industrial processes in which vitamins and minerals are extracted.

Additives: such as preservatives, sweeteners, flavor enhancers, etc.

1. Overweight and obesity

One of the main health problems caused by the excessive consumption of ultra-processed is obesity. Report from WHO, obesity and overweight cases have tripled in recent years. In 2016, 1900 million 18-year-old adults were overweight, of whom 650 million were obese. As if that were not enough, in 2016, 41 million children worldwide were obese or overweight.

2. Cardiovascular disease

Weight gain causes an increased risk of cardiovascular diseases, such as hypertension, arteriosclerosis, myocardial infarction, or stroke. In addition, the excessive consumption of salt present in ultra-processes increases the likelihood of cardiovascular disease. The same happens with monosodium glutamate, an additive that enhances the flavor. According to several studies, an excessive intake favors weight gain, oxidative stress, memory defects, and epilepsy.

3. Diabetes Mellitus type 2

If we regularly consume ultra-processed foods, usually rich in sugars, we can become diabetic. The mechanism is explained because if we take, for example, about 200 grams of sugar daily, insulin is triggered, and glucose cannot enter the cells. It creates an alteration at the metabolic level that can result in insulin resistance.

4. High cholesterol

Another consequence of the excess of ultra-processed foods would be that our blood cholesterol levels could rise by consuming the fat present in this type of product as believed and by sugar. Returning to the previous explanation, insulin resistance implies that the cell cannot open to it. Therefore, glucose begins to accumulate in the arteries. The result would be high blood glucose levels due to hypertension and other heart-related diseases.

5. Cancer

Once you stop consuming a diet low in processed food, your chances of having cancer are very small. However, the reverse is the case when the consumption of highly processed food is a habit.

CHAPTER FIVE

DAY FOUR: WHOLE FOOD IS THE BEST

Whole foods have a range of nutrients that help prevent the appearance of various pathologies. For example, regular consumption of whole foods is linked to a lower risk of some types of cancer, especially colon cancer. Also, studies have shown that it improves reasonable control of diabetes mellitus, especially type 2.

BREAKFAST

BOILED TURKEY

Ingredients

- Turkey breast fillet: 35 oz.

- Salt: As required

- Lemon juice: 3 tsp

- Barbecue Marinade: 3.5 oz.

Preparation

- Make a saline solution: for the 35 oz. of meat, add 1 cup of water, three tablespoons of salt, and lemon juice. Place the breast in the solution for 1 hour.

- Remove the breast from the solution, dry it with a paper towel, rub it with marinade and leave to marinate for 1 hour.

- Preheat the oven to 250 ° C, wrap fillets in foil, place in a baking dish, and place in the oven for 20 minutes. Then, without opening the oven door, turn it off and leave the turkey there until it cools completely - for 2-3 hours.

Nutrition:

- Calories: 86g

- Carb: 23g

- Fat: 2g

- Fiber: 0g

- Protein: 40g

BREADED CHICKEN LEGS

Ingredients

- Coconut flour: 3 tsp

- Almond flour: 1 oz.

- Milk: 2 cups

- Olive oil: 1 cup

- Baking powder: ¼ tsp

- Salt: As required

- Chicken legs: 35 oz.

- Oregano: 0.4 oz.

- Basil: 0.4 oz.

- Cumin: 0.4 oz.

- Garlic: 0.4 oz.

- Pepper: As required

- Two Eggs: 5 oz.

- Frying oil: 1 cup

Preparation

- Stir milk, egg, and olive oil in a cup to produce breadcrumbs. Add almond and coconut flour, baking powder, salt, and blend until smooth. Microwave for 90 seconds. Remove the bread from the cup and slice.

- Heat the oven, arrange bread slices on a baking sheet, and bake for 60-90 minutes or until bread is dry. Grind the bread in a food processor.

- Arrange the breadcrumbs and seasonings on a platter. Mix two eggs into a bowl. Dip each chicken drumstick in eggs, then coat with breadcrumbs.

- Heat oil in a deep skillet. Fry the chicken legs in groups of 12-15 minutes, rotating once or until golden brown.

Nutrition:

- Calories: 197g

- Carb: 20g

- Fat: 4g

- Fiber: 2g

- Protein: 35g

CHICKEN CAPRESE CASSEROLE

Ingredients

- Chicken grill: 20 oz.

- Cherry tomatoes: 7 oz.

- Mozzarella cheese: 7.5 oz.

- Green Pesto Sauce: 3 oz.

- Cream: 7.5 oz.

- Parmesan cheese: 1.7 oz.

- Salt as required

- Pepper as required

- Fresh Basil: 2 oz.

Preparation

- Chop the chicken with a fork, chop the tomatoes, Mozzarella, and place them in a baking dish. Add Pesto, crème fraîche, half Parmesan, salt and pepper, and stir.

- Sprinkle the remaining Parmesan on top and send the future casserole to the oven preheated until golden brown.

Nutrition:

- Calories: 560g

- Carb: 13g

- Fat: 15g

- Fiber: 1g

- Protein: 35g

OVEN-BAKED RICE

Ingredients

- One cup of white rice

- Two cups boiling water

- Salt as required

- One and a half teaspoons of butter

- One teaspoon of a cube of vegetable bouillon

Preparation

- Heat the oven.

- Mix everything in a 2-quart baking dish.

- Bake for 30-40 minutes until all liquid is absorbed and rice is fluffy.

Nutrition:

- Calories: 510g

- Carb: 64g

- Fat: 12g

- Fiber: 4g

- Protein: 12g

BAKED CHICKEN FINGERS & SWEET POTATO FRIES

Ingredients

- Two large sweet potatoes or yams

- 1/2 teaspoons of olive oil

- Salt

- 20 oz of chicken breast

- Low-fat buttermilk: ¼ cup

- Coarsely crushed cornflakes: 1/3 cup

- Seasoned breadcrumbs: 1/3 cup

Preparation

- Preheat the oven to 400°. Use a non-stick cooking spray to rub the baking pan

- Peel sweet potatoes. Slice into French fry-sized pieces.

- Place the potatoes into the baking sheet. Coat potatoes with olive oil and salt. Toss to cover.

- Bake for 20 minutes. Meanwhile, combine chicken and buttermilk in a shallow dish. Cover and chill for 15 minutes.

- Drain chicken, discarding liquid.

- Mix the corn flakes and breadcrumbs in a large zip-top plastic bag.

- Add four chicken pieces to the bag. Seal and shake to coat.

- Repeat the procedure with the remaining chicken.

- Put the Push potatoes on one side of the baking sheet. Arrange chicken in a single layer on the other side.

- Put it inside the oven for about 15-20 minutes, until chicken is cooked through and crisp potatoes.

Nutrition:

- Calories: 340g

- Carb: 69g

- Fat: 23g

- Fiber: 5g

- Protein: 40g

BUTTERNUT SQUASH RISOTTO (IN THE MICROWAVE)

Ingredients

- One cup of uncooked medium-grain rice

- One teaspoon of olive oil

- Two and a half cups fat-free, less-sodium chicken broth

- One cup of water

- Twelve ounces of package frozen pureed butternut squash

- Pinch of salt

- Pinch of black pepper

- Six teaspoons of grated fresh Parmesan cheese

Preparation

- Combine rice and oil in a one 1/2-quart microwave-safe dish, stirring to coat.

- Microwave, uncovered, for 3 minutes.

- Add broth and 1 cup water to the rice mixture. Microwave, uncovered, for 9 minutes.

- Stir well. Microwave, uncovered, for another 6 minutes.

- Remove from the microwave. Wait for 5 minutes or until all liquid is absorbed.

- In the meantime, heat squash in the microwave for 2 minutes or until warm.

- Add squash, salt, pepper, and cheese to risotto. Stir well to combine.

Nutrition:

- Calories: 200g

- Carb: 58g

- Fat: 12g

- Fiber: 3g

- Protein: 15

DINNER

MOCK CHICKEN POT PIE

Ingredients

- 1 ½ cups chicken breast, cooked and diced

- One can diced new potatoes, drained

- 1 cup frozen, sliced carrots

- One can of condensed 98% fat-free cream of chicken soup

- 1/2 cup fat-free milk

- 1 cup Bisquick mix

- 1/2 cup fat-free milk

- One egg: 2 oz.

Preparation

- Preheat the oven to 400 degrees.

- In an ungreased 2-quart casserole dish, mix chicken, vegetables, soup, and 1/2 cup milk.

- Microwave on high for 4 minutes.

- Stir the Bisquick mix, 1/2 cup milk, and the egg with a fork until blended in a small bowl.

- Pour Bisquick mixture over vegetable mixture.

- Bake until golden brown.

Nutrition:

- Calories: 340g

- Carb: 74g

- Fat: 24g

- Fiber: 3g

- Protein: 35g

PITA PIZZA

Ingredients

- 1 cup of Pita

- 3 Tbsp pizza sauce

- 3 Tbsp part-skim (low-fat) mozzarella cheese

- 1 Tbsp grated Parmesan cheese

- Cooked spinach or mushrooms: 2 oz.

- Lean ground turkey, cooked and drained: 10 oz.

- Skinless chicken breast, cooked and shredded: 10 oz.

Preparation

- Heat the toaster oven to 400 degrees.

- Spread sauce on pita.

- Top with desired toppings.

- Sprinkle on cheeses.

- Broil using an oven for 4-5 minutes until the cheese is melted.

Nutrition:

- Calories: 450g

- Carb: 68g

- Fat: 3g

- Fiber: 0.6g

- Protein: 23g

INSTANT POTATO GNOCCHI

Ingredients

This fluffy potato pasta can be eaten with smooth tomato sauce if tolerated.

Ingredients

- 1 cup mashed potato flakes

- 1 cup of boiling water

- One egg: 2 oz.

- 1.5 cups all-purpose flour

- ½ tsp dried basil

- ¼ tsp garlic powder

- 1/8 tsp salt

- 1/8 tsp pepper

- 6 cups of water

Preparation

- In a large bowl, combine potato flakes. Next, combine the boiling water and the egg in a mixing bowl. Finally, add flour and spices and mix to combine.

- Knead 10-12 times on a lightly floured surface until a soft dough forms.

- Divide dough into four equal halves. Roll each half into 12-inch-thick ropes on a floured surface; cut into 34-inch sections.

- With a lightly floured fork, press and roll each piece.

- Bring water to a boil in a big saucepan.

- Gnocchi in batches should be cooked for 39-60 seconds or until they float.

- Remove with a slotted spoon.

- Serve with sauce.

Nutrition:

- Calories: 200g

- Carb: 58g

- Fat: 12g

- Fiber: 3g

- Protein: 15g

PUREES

One of the foods that play a fundamental role in the gastroparesis patients' diet is fruit purees since they will digest faster and prevent protein and nutrient deficiencies. Traditionally, the consumption of purees has been associated with young children or people who have difficulties ingesting solid foods, either due to illness, having problems in the digestive or dental system. In addition, purees are the perfect solution, and experts usually recommend them to people who lack appetite or do not have much time to eat.

HEALTH BENEFITS OF PUREE

- One of the advantages of purees is that they constitute a complete dish for those who do not want to cook. The puree is designed with healthy fats, proteins, vegetables, and legumes.

- It has a reduced cholesterol level. Among the properties attributed to purees is their ability to reduce the chronic consumption of a high cholesterol diet to help our body reduce or prevent a health problem.

- Puree contains a high level of vitamins essential for growth and healthy living. They also play a vital role in the formation of bones and are antioxidants, helping to strengthen your immune system.

- They also provide minerals, such as potassium, great to get the nervous system in the best possible conditions, or magnesium, allowing muscles to function and develop properly.

- It is essential to know that fruit purees help hydrate the body of the little ones since they are foods whose content is formed by approximately 90% water. Therefore, especially in the hottest seasons, such as summer, we must ensure that children are adequately hydrated so that all their organs work properly and do not suffer any type of problem, such as heat stroke.

WHITE SWEET POTATO & ROASTED BANANA

Ingredients

- Sweet potatoes: 20 oz.

- One banana

- 1-2 Tbsp smooth nut butter

- Skim milk: As required

- Rice milk: As required

- Soy milk or almond milk: As required

Preparation

- Preheat the oven to 400 degrees.

- Use a foil to wrap them and place them on a baking sheet. Cook for about 40 minutes.

- Put the banana, peel on, onto the cookie sheet and cook for an additional 15 minutes.

- Allow sweet potatoes and bananas to cool a little, and then remove the peels and skins.

- Use a food processor or blender, adding nut butter if desired and milk as needed to achieve desired consistency.

VEGGIE PUREE

Ingredients

- 1 tsp vegetable oil

- Two carrots, peeled and chopped

- Two sliced leeks, white part only

- Two potatoes, peeled and chopped

- Two parsnips, peeled, chopped

- Two cups of Boiling water

- 4 oz. of green beans

Preparation

- Heat oil in a deep saucepan.

- Add carrots and leeks. Sauté until softened, about 6-7 minutes.

- Add potatoes and parsnips. Add some boiling water until it just covers the veggies.

- Cover and simmer for 15-20 minutes or until veggies are very tender.

- Use either a blender or food processor.

- Stir in baby food green beans, if desired.

SWEET POTATO & CARROT

Ingredients

- One large sweet potato

- One carrot

- ½ cup unsweetened applesauce

- ¼ cup maple syrup, optional

Preparation

- Peel and chop sweet potatoes.

- Cover sweet potato pieces and carrots with water in a large stockpot.

- Bring to a boil over high heat.

- Reduce heat and simmer for about 20-30, until very tender. Remove from heat and drain.

- Combine all ingredients and puree with an immersion blender or a food processor or blender.

ACORN SQUASH & APPLE

Ingredients

- One acorn squash

- 3 Macintosh apples

- 1 tsp cinnamon

- Apple juice: 3 cups

Preparation

- Preheat the oven to 400 degrees.

- Peel and dice apples. Cut acorn squash in half and scoop out seeds.

- In a pan, arrange acorn halves face up. Pour some amount of water into the bottom of the pan.

- Place chopped apples in the "holes" created by the seeds in the squash.

- Sprinkle cinnamon on top.

- Pour enough water over the apples to fill the squash holes.

- Bake for 40 minutes, or until the acorn shell puckers and the apple halves are tender. Cool slightly, then scoop squash "meat" and apples out of the shell.

- Use a blender and add apple juice or water to achieve desired consistency.

SAVORY BUTTERNUT SQUASH & POTATO

Ingredients

- Butternut squash: 48 oz.

- Potatoes, peeled and quartered

- 1 cup evaporated nonfat milk

- 1 Tbsp butter or olive oil

- Salt as required

- Ground black pepper as required

Preparation

- Squash should be cut in half and seeds scooped out. Peel the squash and cut it.

- Add water and salt to the saucepan. Add squash and potatoes.

- Bring to a boil and simmer until the squash and potatoes are soft when pierced with a fork (30-40 minutes).

- Drain the liquid (reserving about 1 cup) and whisk in the milk and butter.

- Puree, adding more cooking liquid as needed to reach desired consistency.

PARSNIP & POTATO

Ingredients

- 2 Russet potatoes

- Two large parsnips

- Chicken broth: 5 oz.

Preparation

- Peel and chop potatoes and parsnips into small pieces.

- In a large stockpot, cover potato and parsnip pieces with water.

- Bring to a boil over high heat.

- Reduce heat for about 20-30 minutes.

- Remove from heat and drain.

- Run through a potato ricer –or– puree using an immersion blender, food processor, or blender, adding broth as needed until desired consistency is achieved.

Ingredients

- One carrot, peeled and cut

- Two peeled turnips

- 1/2 cup yogurt

- 1/4 tsp ground ginger

- 1 Tbsp softened butter, optional

- Salt as required

- Pepper as required

Preparation

- Cook both carrots and turnips in boiling salted water for 30 to 40 minutes or until tender.

- Remove water and place it into a food processor.

- Add yogurt, ground ginger, and softened butter. Process until smooth.

- Season with salt and pepper to taste.

Ingredients

- Six large red potatoes

- Two large turnips

- 1/2 cup chicken broth, warmed

- 1/2 cup nonfat sour cream

- Salt as required

- Pepper as required

Preparation

- Peel and thinly slice potatoes and turnips.

- Cook for 15-20 minutes or until fork-tender in boiling water. Drain.

- Using an electric mixer, whip boiled potatoes and turnips until smooth.

- Add warm chicken broth and sour cream/yogurt.

- Season with salt and pepper to taste. Whip again until blended

SOUPS

A hot soup dish is essential for cold or rainy days, especially for gastroparesis patients. These foods help the body's systems. Because soups and broths are mostly composed of water, they are meals that aid in maintaining sufficient hydration while also being low in calories. The main ingredients for soup include vegetables, fish, meat, pasta, legumes, rice, condiments, etc.

Health Benefits of Soups

- It provides very significant amounts of nutrients (vitamins and minerals).

- It has protective substances for our bodies.

- It is very easy to digest.

- It is a good source of hydration.

- Soup increases bile production at the beginning of a meal and lowers cholesterol levels.

- Consumed at the beginning of the meal, it also promotes the gradual release of insulin, stimulating appetite and satiating you early and continuously.

- Unlike other culinary preparations, it does not have significant amounts of naturally occurring toxins, anti-nutritions, or allergens.

- Depending on the ingredients it has, it can be more or less caloric, more or less moisturizing, have more or less salt, and have more or less fiber. This flexibility makes soup the ideal food for any age and any state of health.

- The soup is still a type of economical confection, relatively fast, and can be prepared in advance to be heated and served only on time.

EASY CHICKEN NOODLE SOUP

Ingredients

- 2 tsp butter

- 1 cup chopped carrots

- 1/2 cup chopped onions (if tolerated)

- Two potatoes, diced

- 1 tsp thyme

- 1 tsp poultry seasoning

- Four cups of chicken broth

- 2 tsp chicken bouillon

- 4 ounces egg noodles (uncooked)

- 2 cups cooked chicken breast, chopped

Preparation

- Melt butter in a large pot.

- Sauté the carrot and onion for 2 minutes.

- Heat the potato, thyme, poultry spice, chicken broth, and bouillon.

- Cook on low for 20 minutes, then add noodles and chicken.

Ingredients

- 5-6 large potatoes

- ½ cup chopped onion

- 32 oz. of chicken broth (reserve one cup for gravy)

Preparation

- Combine all ingredients except gravy mix and 1 cup of broth in a large pot.

- In a separate container, stir together gravy mix and reserved broth.

- Lower the heat for about an hour until potatoes are very tender and soup has thickened.

EGG-LEMON SOUP

Ingredients

- 6 cups chicken broth

- 3/4 cup uncooked white rice or orzo pasta

- Three eggs: 7 oz.

- 3 cups of lemon juice

Preparation

- Bring broth to boil in a saucepan.

- Add rice or orzo. Cover and cook on medium-low heat for 20-25 minutes (rice) or 10 minutes

- While the rice is cooking, whisk together the eggs and lemon juice.

- Remove the rice/pasta from the heat after the rice/pasta is done.

- Slowly incorporate about one cup of the heated broth into the egg/lemon combination.

- Add the egg/lemon/broth combination to the soup in a slow, steady stream, stirring frequently.

- Reintroduce the pot to heat and whisk until the soup is thoroughly heated.

POTATO SPINACH SOUP

Well-cooked spinach is often tolerated without blending, but this soup can easily be pureed. In addition, this recipe uses no broth, which makes it lower in sodium than many other soup recipes.

Ingredients

- 1 tbsp butter

- ½ large onion (if tolerated)

- ¼ cup flour

- 3 cups water

- 2 cups potatoes, peeled and cubed

- 2 tsp salt

- 1 cup spinach, chopped (fresh or frozen)

- 1/2 cup evaporated skim milk

Preparation

- Melt butter in a pan.

- Add onions. Cook for about 15 minutes.

- Blend in flour, and cook for a couple of minutes.

- Add potatoes, water, and salt. Stir constantly until boiling.

- Reduce heat and simmer for 30 minutes.

- Add spinach. Cook for an additional 5-6 minutes until spinach is very well cooked.

- Pureed, if desired, using an immersion blend, food processor, or blender.

- Gradually stir in milk.

BLENDED BEET & POTATO SOUP

Ingredients

- Four medium-sized beets, peeled and cooked

- Four medium-sized potatoes, and peeled

- ½ tsp of chopped onion

- 1 tsp dried dill

- 1 Tbsp butter

- 8 cups vegetable stock

- 1/2 cup fat-free evaporated milk or dairy-free substitute

- Salt as required

- Pepper as required

Preparation

- Sauté onions with dill in butter until softened.

- Add cubed potatoes, stock, and beets.

- Cook until veggies are very soft, about 30-40 minutes.

- Blend until smooth with an immersion blender.

- Stir in milk. Add salt and pepper to taste.

PUREED CARROT & GINGER SOUP

Ingredients

- 2 tsp canola oil

- ½ tsp of chopped onion

- 3 tbsp finely chopped fresh ginger root

- 3 cups carrots, chopped

- One medium potato, peeled and chopped

- 8 cups vegetable or chicken stock

- Salt as required

- Nutmeg as required

Preparation

- Heat the oil in a large pot.

- Add the onion and ginger, and sauté until the onion is translucent.

- Add the carrots, potato, and vegetable stock.

- Cook until the vegetables are very tender

- Purée in batches in a blender or food processor

- Add salt and nutmeg. Serve alone or over white rice.

SMOOTHIES

Fruit smoothies may help you enhance your health, and they offer your diverse body kinds of nutrients. Consuming natural meals such as fruits and vegetables may improve brain function and healthy weight reduction. As if that weren't enough, it can also help strengthen your immune system, allowing your body to battle a wider variety of ailments. Here are some of the advantages of smoothies for gastroparesis patients:

HEALTH BENEFITS OF SMOOTHIES

Boost your immune system:

If you drink fruit smoothies regularly, you can boost your immune system and have more defenses in your body to fight against foreign bodies that can make you sick. In addition, fruits will also help your brain be stronger and more receptive to information.

Cleanse your body:

Fruit smoothies are full of antioxidants, and these help you make your body cleaner and free of toxins. In addition, your digestive system will also look strengthened and cleaner.

You'll sleep better:

By having a cleaner body, you will be healthier, you will feel healthier, and therefore, you will sleep better. If you have trouble sleeping, drinking fruit smoothies can be a way to feel much better.

You will have more energy:

If you take fruit smoothies regularly, you can have more energy. You will feel much better emotionally and also in your emotional state. But don't forget that fruit smoothies should be supplemented with a healthy, balanced diet and physical activity time.

You will lose weight

The good thing about fruit is that it can satisfy your hunger between meals, you will be eating, and you will do it healthily. This is especially ideal for losing weight or when you want to cleanse your body. Fruit smoothies can be a great ally for you to lose weight.

You will have much more radiant skin:

Fruits and their antioxidants will help you have much more radiant skin. It will also improve the nails, and you will have much stronger hair, and it will grow more often.

You will enjoy a healthy diet:

It is not advisable to use fruit smoothies as a replacement for meals, but this can be done to purify your body for one day. To maintain good health and get all vital minerals and vitamins, your body needs a diverse and balanced diet. The fruit smoothie is great for a snack or a mid-morning meal.

You will be able to make many combinations:

The best thing is also that you currently have many fruits available so it will be very easy for you to find varieties of fruits that go well and that you like. You can discover many new flavors and enjoy delicious smoothies.

BASIC SMOOTHIE RECIPE

Mix and match the following basic ingredients based on your preferences and dietary tolerances. If you can't tolerate dairy products, omit the yogurt and increase the liquid to 1 cup. Any type of liquid can be used, including cow's milk, soy milk, almond milk, rice milk, or juice.

- ½ cup of plain or vanilla Greek yogurt

- ½ cup of juice, milk, or milk substitute

- 1 cup frozen fruit

Preparation

- Blend all ingredients until smooth.

- Add liquid until it reaches desired consistency.

NUTTY PEANUT BUTTER & BANANA SMOOTHIE

Ingredients

- One banana, sliced and frozen

- 6-8 oz. milk or almond milk

- 1 Tbsp peanut butter

- 2 tbsp of cinnamon

Preparation

- Blend all ingredients until smooth.

NOTE: Some gastroparesis patients tolerate high-fat liquids very well, and this particular smoothie is ideal for those who need to gain or maintain weight. To reduce the fat content, use skims, soy, rice, or almond milk, adding a splash of coconut extract to keep the tropical flavor.

PEACHY-KEEN KEFIR SMOOTHIE

Kefir is a cultured, enzyme-rich beverage filled with healthy bacteria (probiotics). It also supplies complete protein, essential minerals, and B vitamins. Choose organic whenever possible.

Ingredients

- 1 cup of kefir

- 1 cup of peaches, canned or frozen

Preparation

- Blend until smooth.

Pumpkin has considerable fiber but is often easily tolerated when pureed and diluted.

Ingredients

- 1/2 cup canned pumpkin (or four oz. jar of baby food squash)

- 1/2 frozen banana

- 3/4 cup almond milk

- 1/2 scoop (about 2 Tbsp) vanilla protein powder

- 1 tsp pumpkin pie spice

Preparation

- Bring a blender and put all ingredients

- Blend thoroughly until smooth.

- Add water or more almond milk, if needed, until the mixture reaches the desired consistency.

STRAWBERRIES & CREAM SIPPER

This is a very tasty little pick-me-up with a good amount of vitamins B6, B12, and C. It has quite a bit of sugar, though, so enjoy it in moderation.

Ingredients

- 3 oz. Bolthouse Farms Strawberry Banana Smoothie

- 3 oz. Bolthouse Farms Vanilla Chai Smoothie

- 2-4 oz. water

Preparation

- Mix all ingredients

- Refrigerate.

SAFE & SIMPLE STRAWBERRY SMOOTHIE

Many gastroparesis patients avoid berries due to the seeds and skins. The strawberry juice drinks used in this recipe are a great alternative as they are pulp-free. This low-fat, low fiber "recipe" has about 7 grams of protein and provides a significant amount of vitamins B6, B12, and C. Best of all, and it's really tasty.

Ingredients

- 4 oz. Strawberry

- 2 oz. water

- A few ice cubes

Preparation

- Blend the juices and ice in a blender

- Add as much water as necessary to reach desired consistency.

- Variation: for a thinner drink, combine the juices in a glass with about 4 ounces of water and add a few ice cubes.

GP-FRIENDLY GREEN MONSTER

Ingredients

- Four cups of apple juice

- Two cups of carrot juice

- One cup of cucumber juice

- One cup of kale juice

- Half cup of banana juice

Preparation

- Peel and banana the apples.

- Peel the carrots and cucumber.

- Wash the kale.

- Put all the fruits and veggies in an electric juicer.

- Collect the juice in a measuring cup to know when you have the appropriate amount of each juice. Add the kale first; the other fruits will push extra kale juice out of the machine.

- Strain the juice really well to remove any pulp.

- Put a small fine-mesh strainer over the cup that you use to collect the juice. Then pour the juice through the strainer again when adding it to the blender.

- Combine juice, fish oil, and banana/ice in a blender and blend until smooth.

EASIER GREEN MONSTER

Unlike the original Green Monster smoothie, this one doesn't require a juicer. It still provides a good amount of vitamins and phytonutrients, though. The Greek yogurt is optional but will add about 6 grams of protein. The fish oil, which you can't taste at all, adds 4.5 grams of healthy Omega-3 fat. This recipe yields about 2 cups, so you may want to freeze half for another day.

Ingredients

- Water: 2 cups

- Carrot Juice: 2 cups

- Green: 3 oz

- Banana: 4 oz

- Greek or regular yogurt: 1 cup

Preparation

- Blend all ingredients until smooth.

SNACKS & TREATS

When you hear the word snack, you're likely to think of chips and cookies, which may lead you to think this is something to avoid. However, eating between meals can be good for you if you make healthy choices, and older people might need a snack to make up for eating less at meals.

If you eat less at each meal, it can be difficult to get the necessary energy, vitamins, and minerals with just three meals a day. However, having a snack, or eating six mini meals a day instead of just 3, can fill in the gaps.

Nutrients Contain in Snacks

A vitamin- and nutrient-dense diet may help prevent illness and support your whole body, from your bones to your heart. In addition, experts suggest using snack time to increase your intake of the following, which could be missing from an older person's diet:

Vitamin B12: The deficiency of this nutrient can lead to anemia, and older people are especially at risk. Heartburn is when the stomach decreases with age, making it harder for the body to absorb vitamin B12. In addition, fortified cereals, yogurt, eggs, and lean meat are high in vitamin B12.

Vitamin D is critical for bone health; your body needs sunlight to produce this nutrient. Salmon is a rich source of vitamin D, and milk, yogurt, and eggs are also good sources.

Fiber: Fruits and vegetables, whole grains and whole-grain bread and cereals, nuts, and beans are rich in fiber. For example, you can find soluble fiber in apples, beans, and oatmeal, among other foods.

Protein: Muscle mass naturally decreases with age, making you more prone to falls and decreasing your ability to perform daily activities. Protein is crucial to preserve it. Instead of consuming protein only at one meal, eat a portion at least three times a day.

Potassium: It helps the proper functioning of the heart and kidneys. You find it abundantly in bananas, plums, beans, potatoes, sweet potatoes, yogurt, and fish.

People think of snacks as prepackaged products, like potato chips," Morse says. Here is a list of snacks to consume as a gastroparesis patient.

GP-FRIENDLY BROWNIE FOR ONE

Ingredients

- 2 tbsp flour

- 2 tbsp sugar

- 1 tbsp unsweetened cocoa powder

- 1/8 tsp baking powder

- 2 tbsp applesauce or nonfat or low-fat yogurt

- 1 tbsp milk or water

Preparation

- Stir together flour, sugar, cocoa powder, and baking powder in a small bowl.

- Add applesauce/yogurt and milk/water. Mix just until combined.

- Microwave for about 50 seconds or until set. The center will still look a bit gooey.

- Allow to cool slightly but eat while still warm.

BAKED BANANAS

Bananas tend to be well-tolerated by many GOPers and are a good potassium and vitamin B6 source. So, if you're tired of banana smoothies, give this recipe a try instead.

Ingredients

- Four firm bananas

- Non-stick cooking spray

- Half tsp dried ginger

- 1 Tbsp cinnamon

- 1/2 Tbsp nutmeg

- 1/4 cup maple syrup, optional

Preparation

- Preheat the oven to 375 degrees.

- Peel and cut bananas in half, lengthwise.

- Use non-stick cooking spray on the pan

- Arrange bananas in a single layer.

- Drizzle with maple syrup. Sprinkle it with cinnamon, nutmeg, and ginger.

- Bake for 10 to 15 minutes.

- Mash or puree cooked bananas if desired.

EASY PUMPKIN MUFFINS

Ingredients

- One cup of spice cake mix

- One solid-pack pumpkin

- 1/2 tsp vanilla

- 1/2 tsp cinnamon

Preparation

- Preheat the oven to 350 degrees.

- Spray the muffin pan using a cooking spray.

- Mix cake, pumpkin, cinnamon, and vanilla in a large bowl. An electric mixer is helpful since the mixture is very thick. However, don't overwork the dough, or the muffins will be tough.

- Fill muffin cups 2/3 full. (If you have a medium-sized ice cream scoop, it makes this really easy.)

- Bake for about 22 minutes until a toothpick inserted into one of the muffins comes out clean.

- Let cool for about 10 minutes.

Prepare the glaze with the following Ingredients

- 1 cup powdered sugar

- 2-3 tbsp apple cider

- 1/2 tsp pumpkin pie spice

Preparation

1. Combine all ingredients.

2. Spoon glaze over the warm muffins.

BAKED PUMPKIN PUDDING

This is basically a crustless pumpkin pie. It's perfect for Thanksgiving or Christmas.

Ingredients

- One cup of solid-pack pumpkin puree
- One cup of evaporated skim milk
- 3/4 cup white sugar
- Half cup Bisquick baking mix
- Two eggs: 5 oz
- 1 tbsp butter, melted
- 2 ½ tsp pumpkin pie spice
- ¼ tsp of grounded ginger
- 2 tsp vanilla extract

Preparation

- Preheat the oven to 350 degrees.
- Put all ingredients in a blender and blend until combined.
- Pour into the pie pan.
- Bake in a preheated oven for 50 to 55 minutes, or until a knife inserted in the center comes out clean.

CROCKPOT RICE PUDDING

While this is technically a desert, I happen to think rice pudding also makes a yummy breakfast during the winter months.

Ingredients

- ¾ cup of short-grain rice

- 12 oz. of evaporated skim milk

- 2 cups of water

- 1/3 cup of white sugar

- 1 ½ tsp of vanilla

- ½ tsp of ground cinnamon

Preparation

- Mix all ingredients and stir well.

- Cook for about 2 hours.

- Stir twice during the cooking process.

LOW FAT BANANA BREAD

Ingredients

- 2 cups of all-purpose flour

- 3/4 tsp of baking soda

- 1/2 tsp of salt

- 1 cup of sugar

- 1/4 cup of butter

- Half cup of egg substitute

- One and a half mashed ripe banana

- 1/3 cup of non-fat Greek yogurt or plain low-fat yogurt

- 1 tsp of vanilla extract

Preparation

- Preheat the oven to 350°F. Spray a bread pan with cooking spray.

- Blend the flour, baking soda, and salt in a bowl.

- Beat butter and sugar in a large bowl until well combined, about 1 minute.

- Mix in egg substitute, mashed bananas, yogurt, and vanilla.

- Add flour mixture to banana mixture. Mix until combined.

- Bake until it is lightly brown and a toothpick inserted into the center comes out clean.

- Cool for a few minutes in a pan. Then remove the bread from the pan and cool completely.

MARSHMALLOW CEREAL TREATS

Ingredients

- 3 tbsp of butter

- 10 ounces of mini-marshmallows

- 1 tsp of vanilla extract

- 5 cups of low-fat, and low-fiber cereal

Preparation

- Spray a 9x9 pan with cooking spray.

- Melt butter.

- Add marshmallows.

- Cook and stir until marshmallows are melted.

- Remove from heat. Stir in vanilla.

- Add cereal and stir until combined.

- Immediately pour into the prepared pan.

- Allow cooling before cutting.

A great dessert for company, this cake can be served to others with mashed berries and fresh whipped cream on the side.

Ingredients

- Sifted cake flour: 2 oz.

- Unsweetened cocoa: 1 cup

- Granulated sugar: 0.5 oz.

- Egg: 4 oz.

- Vanilla extract: 2 oz.

- Cream of tartar: 0.5

- Salt as required

Preparation

- Preheat the oven to 375 degrees.

- Sift together flour, cocoa, and 3/4 cup granulated sugar; set aside.

- Beat egg whites until frothy.

- Combine vanilla, cream of tartar, and salt in a small bowl.

- Add remaining sugar gradually.

- When the sugar is integrated, continue beating for approximately 2 minutes more or until firm peaks form.

- Filter the dry ingredients; fold in gently using a rubber spatula. Reverse the process until all dry ingredients are combined.

- Pour batter into a 10-inch tube pan that has not been oiled.

- Bake until the top springs back softly when pushed.

- Invert the pan and hang it from the neck of a bottle or set it on its side to cool.

- Run a thin knife along the pan's and tube's sides to unmold.

BIG, CHEWY GINGER COOKIES

Ingredients

- 2 cups white flour

- 2 tsp baking soda

- Salt as required

- 2 tsp ground ginger

- 1 tsp ground cinnamon

- One ¼ cup brown sugar

- 2 Tbsp butter

- ¼ cup molasses

- Two large eggs: 7 oz.

- ½ cup unsweetened applesauce

Preparation

- Preheat your oven to 325°F.

- Combine all of the ingredients from the flour through the brown sugar and mix well.

- Using an electric mixer, combine the butter, molasses, egg whites, and applesauce.

- Input the dry ingredients to the wet mixture and mix well.

- Spray a baking sheet with non-stick spray.

- Drop the batter by 1 1/2 tablespoons onto the baking sheet.

- The cookies will spread, so allow some room.

- Bake till it brown on the bottom.

- Cool on a rack.

CHOCOLATE CINNAMON MERINGUES

These pretty, crunchy cookies are fat-free, fiber-free, and gluten-free.

Ingredients

- 1 cup of sugar

- 1/3 cup of cocoa powder

- Four eggs: 12 oz.

- 1/2 tsp of ground cinnamon

- 1/4 tsp of cream of tartar

Preparation

- Sift together the sugar and cocoa powder. Mix the egg whites, cinnamon, and cream of tartar using an electric mixer.

- Add the sugar mixture.

- At high speed, beat the whole mixture until glossy and firm.

- Preheat oven to 350°F. Line two baking pans with parchment paper.

- Bake for 40–45 minutes at 250 degrees F, or until the tops feel dry to the touch.

- Allow 5 minutes for cooling before removing from parchment paper.

A healthier, no-marshmallow version of rice crispy treats. However, peanut butter boosts the fat content, so watch your portion size.

Ingredients

- 1/3 cup of smooth peanut butter

- 1/3 cup of honey

- 3 cups of brown rice crispy cereal

- 1 tsp of vanilla extract

Preparation

- Use a baking dish and line it with parchment paper.

- Put peanut butter, rice syrup/honey, and vanilla into a small saucepan.

- Use low heat for cooking until the mixture is warm and melty.

- Add the rice cereal to the bowl.

- Spread the peanut butter mixture over the cereal and stir until all of the cereal is coated.

- Spread cereal mixture into the baking dish in an even layer.

- Place in the refrigerator for about an hour before serving.

APPLE CINNAMON COFFEE CAKE

Ingredients

- 1/4 cup of sugar

- 2 tsp of cinnamon

- One cup of organic white or yellow cake mix

- 1 2/3 cup of cinnamon applesauce

- 3/4 cup of egg substitute

Preparation

- Preheat the oven to 350 degrees.

- Homogenize the sugar and cinnamon in a small bowl.

- Spray a 10-inch tube pan or bundt pan with cooking spray.

- Dust pan with the sugar and cinnamon mixture.

- Stir together cake mix, applesauce, and egg beaters until well combined.

- Bake for 40-45 minutes

CHAPTER SIX

DAY FIVE - DAY SIX: LIVING HEALTHY

As a gastroparesis patient, you must be aware of your daily diet, which will ensure that you prioritize and plan your meals carefully. In addition, you should lead a better lifestyle to have greater physical and mental well-being, whether with great or small efforts. Certain types of food mustn't be found in your kitchen, and also, regular exercise should be done. The truth is that gastroparesis patients look healthier when combining good food and regular exercise. In this chapter, you shall learn how to live healthy without causing any harm to yourself.

BREAKFAST

PIZZA DOUGH RECIPE

Ingredients

- Wheat flour: 14 oz.

- Baker's yeast: 1 tsp

- Water: 3 cups

- Salt: As required

- Sugar: As required

- Vegetable oil: 2 tbsp

Preparation

- First of all, in a large plastic container, mix the yeast and water. Then add the two tablespoons of vegetable oil. Mix everything with your fingers and start incorporating the wheat flour, little by little. Then add the pinch of salt and the pinch of sugar.

- At first, the dough will stick unbearably on your fingers, but stay patient. Continue to mix the ingredients and add flour, little by little.

- It would help if you continued to knead it with both hands until the moment when it would stop sticking to your fingers. It will take several minutes.

- Then place the pizza dough in its plastic container and cover it with a clean cloth. Let it sit for 1 hour. In addition, the dough will increase in volume.

- Once the hour has passed, you will surely find that the dough has grown. Ideally, it will have doubled in volume.

- Spread the pizza dough and place it on the flat surface where you worked it before, with a little more flour.

- Ensure that you knead the dough again to form a ball shape for about five minutes. Then stretch it little by little. You'll try to get the classic round shape of a pizza, or a square or rectangular shape, depending on your taste and the shape of your pizza tray. You can work on it with the help of a roller.

- Place the dough on its tray when you have achieved the desired size. Once the dough is well distributed on the tray, let it sit for another 5 minutes. You can take this time to prepare the pizza ingredients and to preheat the oven to 200 degrees (Celsius).

PANCAKE DOUGH

Ingredients

- Wheat flour: 1 tbsp

- Baking powder: 1 tsp

- Vanilla extract: 1 tsp

- An egg: 3.5 oz.

- One cup of milk

- Sugar: 1 tsp

- Salt: As required

- Butter or vegetable oil: As required

Instructions:

- To start, place all the ingredients in a medium bowl and mix them well with an electric mixer.

- Ensure the materials are put into a blender or food processor. The result will be the same, but you will get it faster.

- It would help if you got a slightly thick mixture but easy to mix with a spoon. Suppose you want to reduce or dilute the mixture; you can add a little more milk or flour, depending on your needs.

- Then heat a pan over medium. Add a drop of oil or a little butter.

- Then take a tablespoon and use it as a measure. One spoon of pancake batter = 1 pancake.

- To continue, simply fill your tablespoon with the pancake batter and pour it carefully over the bottom of the pan, trying to distribute it circularly.

- Afterward, let the pancake cook until bubbles form on its surface, which means it is already cooked on one side.

- Using a kitchen spatula, gently turn your pancake over and let it cook on the other side for up to 2 minutes.

- Ensure that you remove it from the pan and place it on a plate once it is over.

- Repeat the same procedure until you exhaust the pancake batter. Each time you remove a cooked pancake from the pan, place it on the others, on the same plate. Stacking your pancakes will help keep them warm.

CINNAMON BUNS:

We will classify into three parts the ingredients that can allow you to prepare your homemade cinnamon brioche. You will first have the ingredients for the dough, then for the filling, and finally for the icing.

Ingredients for brioche dough

- Two teaspoons of salt

- Two eggs: 5 oz.

- A cup of warm milk

- 1/2 cup sugar

- 1/2 cup melted butter

- Four cups of bread flour

- One cup of active dry yeast

Ingredients for the cinnamon filling

- A cup of brown sugar

- Grounded cinnamon

- 1/2 cup softened butter.

Ingredients for icing

- Half a cup of cream cheese

- 1/4 cup softened butter

- 1/8 teaspoon salt

- 1 1/2 cups icing sugar

- 1/2 teaspoon vanilla

Preparation

Step 1: Elaboration of the brioche dough

- You get the butter from the refrigerator, and you cut it into pieces and leave it at room temperature for 10 min.

- Take the large bowl and put the yeast and sugar in it.

- You can also add a little milk.

- Gently stir the mixture to allow the yeast to activate.

- Once the yeast is activated, add the eggs, salt, and flour.

- It is important that the flour completely covers the mixture.

- Start mixing all these ingredients to have a firm and elastic paste. You need to knead for about 15 minutes until homogeneous. You can add a little flour or a spoonful of milk soup as needed to obtain the desired consistency by kneading.

- Now add the butter. It should be at 14 °C to avoid overheating the dough. You knead again for about 4 min until it incorporates the dough correctly.

- It is recalled that the procedure is the same if you use a kneading robot, but it is faster.

- Place the dough on a lightly floured surface and cover it with a clean cloth or food plastic film. This is to ensure that the formation of a crust is avoided.

- Then you leave it to rest for at least 30 minutes. It all depends on the ambient temperature. Normally, if all the steps are well followed, the dough should double in volume.

Step 2: Preparation of the cinnamon filling

- You spread the dough over a large, lightly floured area and give it the shape of a rectangle of about 40x50cm with a thickness of 1/4 inch.

- Apply the softened butter to the dough.

- Mix the brown sugar and cinnamon.

- Sprinkle the buttered dough abundantly with the sugar-cinnamon mixture.

- Ensure to roll the dough starting from the longest side to form a dough log.

- Cut into 12 slices of the same thickness.

- Install the resulting slices on a greased cookie sheet or baking sheet.

Step 3: Cooking and icing cinnamon rolls

- Let the buns grow on the baking sheet for thirty minutes. Also, you need to preheat the oven to 400°F (200°C). Then you cook the buns for about 15 to 20 minutes.

- While cooking, prepare the cream cheese icing by beating the butter, icing sugar, cream cheese, vanilla, and salt. You will now remove the buns from the oven and spread the mixture in it. Let your homemade cinnamon buns cool down a bit and serve yourself.

QUICHE LORRAINE

Ingredients

- Four eggs: 10 oz.

- Fresh cream: 8 oz.

- Milk: 2 oz.

- Bacon: 6 oz.

- A teaspoon of butter

- Salt: As required

- Pepper: As required

- Broken dough

Instructions

- Preheat the oven to 185 ° C, preferably with rotating heat.

- Flour a table to spread the quiche dough with the help of a rolling pin.

- Then place the dough on a quiche pan and make the necessary pressure to adapt it to its shape.

- Then, cut out the leftover dough longer than the edge of the mold, if that's the case.

- Bake the container with the dough for 15 minutes.

- Once the time has elapsed, take the dough out of the oven.

- Prepare the mixture for your quiche when the dough is baking to make the most of the time. First, cut the bacon into small cubes

- Then heat a saucepan.

- Then, fry the bacon. The idea is to get a soft texture, not crispy.

- While the bacon cooks, beat the eggs in a container, then add the milk and cream—season with salt and pepper.

- Remove the bacon from its pan and "dry" it using sheets of absorbent paper.

- After removing the broken dough from the oven, pour half of the bacon, covering the bottom. Do not turn off the oven.

- Then cover the bacon with the mixture of eggs, cream, and milk.

- Then, pour what's left of the bacon.

- So, bake it all. Cook your quiche for about 30 minutes or until the surface turns golden.

QUICHE WITH CHEESE AND HAM

Ingredients for quiche dough

- Cold butter: 5.5 oz.

- Sugar: 0.5 oz.

- Salt: As required

- One egg: 3 oz.

- Wheat flour: 8 oz.

- Coldwater: 4 cups

Ingredients for the filling of the cheese and ham quiche

- Creme fraiche: 3.5 oz.

- Two eggs: 4 oz.

- Ham: 3.5 oz.

- Grated Emmental: 5.3 oz.

- Parmesan cheese: 2 oz.

Instructions

How to make easy quiche dough:

- In a food processor, place the cold butter cut into cubes, along with flour, salt, and sugar. Mix with short and fast movements.

- Then the egg and water should be added to the mixture without much movement, making the dough elastic.

- Remember not to work the dough.

- After a reasonable period of refrigeration, remove the dough from the refrigerator. So, cover your table with a little flour, and then spread the dough with a roll.

- If necessary, cut the dough according to the size of your quiche containers. Cover them with dough on the inside side. Remove pieces that remain longer than the edges of the containers.

- This is the time to freeze the containers covered with quiche dough.

- Once frozen, you will take your containers out of the freezer. Place somewhat heavy elements in the center of the container, such as grains. These will have the function of holding the center of your dough stuck to the bottom of the container.

- Bring your containers to the oven preheated to 180-190 ° C.

- When the edges of your quiche dough begin to take on the color of the baked dough, remove the heavy objects from the center of the containers. When cooking continues, watch your pasta so that it does not swell. If it still happens to you, deflate them with a spoon.

- You have to take the quiche pasta out of the oven when it looks cooked, but not golden!

Preparation of the filling of the quiche with cheese and ham

- Mix all the ingredients of the filling: ham, cheese, fresh cream, eggs, and a pinch of salt and pepper to taste.

- Then simply fill the containers with the previously cooked dough with the filling ingredients.

- Cover everything with Parmesan cheese to get a quiche gratinée.

- Bring your preparation to the oven for 20 minutes, at 200 degrees.

- Once the time is up, take your quiches out of the oven.

SCRAMBLED EGGS

Ingredients

- Four eggs: 12 oz.

- Olive oil: 3 cups

- Salt: As required

- Ground black pepper: As required

- Coriander: 4 oz.

Preparation

- In a pan, pour some amount of olive oil

- Pour the eggs and add salt, pepper, and coriander. Mix everything very well. Once everything is mixed, light the fire gently.

- With plastic or wooden pallets, mix the ingredients non-stop. If the eggs begin to become overcooked, remove them from the heat and continue to mix them. Above all, do not let them dry.

- The eggs will be ready when the gelatinous texture of the egg whites disappears.

OATMEAL PANCAKES

Ingredients

- ½ cup of oatmeal in flakes

- Three eggs: 6 oz.

- Two spoons of skim milk

- Salt: As required

- Sweetener or Sugar: As required

- Vegetable oil: 2 cups

Preparation

- First, beat the egg and the three whites in a bowl. Then add the oats, salt, and sweetener and mix well with an electric mixer.

- Then, add the skim milk. If you find that your mixture does not yet have enough consistency, you can add a few more oats.

- You can add half a banana previously cut into small pieces. This gives a touch of flavor and an incredible texture.

- Then heat a pan over medium heat. Add a very small amount of vegetable oil. In fact, in this case, it is pancakes without butter.

- Take the mixture and pour it evenly over the heated pan with a tablespoon.

- Then, cook until bubbles begin to form on the surface of the pancake.

- Finally, repeat this process until you finish all the mixing.

CHICKEN RICE

Ingredients

- Chopped Chicken: 15 oz.

- Two cups of rice

- Four cups of chicken broth

- Tomatoes: As required

- 1/2 teaspoon of red pepper

- Four teaspoons of corn

- Chorizo: 4 oz.

- Onion: As required

- Two cloves of garlic: 2 oz.

- Black olives: 5 oz.

- Cooked Chickpeas: 4 tbsp

- Olive oil: 2 cups

- Salt: As required

- Pepper: As required

Preparation

1. Cut and peel the onion and garlic into very small pieces. Also, cut the tomato and chili pepper, already well washed. In the case of chili, you remove the seeds and internal white parts.

2. Then cut the chorizo into slices or small pieces. If you wish, you can cut the olives into slices or leave them whole if they have no pits.

3. In a pot or paella pan, pour a drizzle of olive oil and sauté the garlic, onion, pepper, chili, chorizo, olives, and finally, the tomato. Add small salt to enhance the flavors and reserve all this mixture in a bowl.

4. In the same pan or pan you used to sauté the first ingredients, add a little more olive oil and sauté the chicken pieces—brown them on all sides. After a few minutes, return the other previously cooked ingredients to the saucepan. Then, mix it all up.

5. Then add the 2 cups of white rice, mix well and pour the 4 cups of chicken broth. Then add a small teaspoon of salt, a touch of pepper to taste, and a teaspoon of yellow food coloring.

6. Finally, add the corn kernels and peas. Mix everything again to distribute the chicken, rice, and vegetables in the paella pan, and then let them boil at rest.

7. When the liquid is almost completely evaporated, reduce the heat to a minimum and cover the pan or pan—Cook the chicken rice for 20 minutes.

8. Taste the rice and if the texture and consistency of the grain are already good, remove the preparation from the heat and serve it. Garnish each dish with a drizzle of olive oil.

Ingredients

- 2 cups white rice

- Fresh shrimp: 17 oz.

- Coconut milk: 8 oz.

- 6 cups shrimp broth

- Tomatoes: 0.5 oz.

- A medium onion: 2 oz.

- Two cloves garlic: 2 oz.

- A piece of the lemongrass stalk: 3 oz.

- A piece of ginger: 0.5 oz.

- A tablespoon of chiseled fresh coriander

- Pepper: As required

- Salt: As required

- Olive oil: 2 cups

Preparation

- To begin, remove the skins and heads from the shrimp, to use them to prepare the broth.

- Place the heads and skins of the shrimp in a deep saucepan. Add water until you double the volume of shrimp remains.

- Boil your preparation and once boiling, reduce the intensity of the heat to half, cover the pan and cook the whole thing for 25 minutes.

- Once this time has elapsed, crush the shrimp remains with a spatula or a large spoon to bring maximum taste to your broth. Then pass the preparation to the filter to preserve only the liquid.

- Reserve the broth necessary to make this recipe and prepare your vegetables. You can taste the broth to check the seasoning and, if necessary, rectify it with a little salt or pepper.

- If you have not yet cut the coriander, wash it well, take only the leaves, and cut them very thinly until you get a tablespoon.

- Chop the onion and the tomato.

- Peel the garlic cloves and cut them very finely.

- Also, peel the ginger and grate it.

- Finally, wash the lemongrass and copy it very finely.

- To continue, take another saucepan a little deep, and heat it over medium heat. Add a drizzle of olive oil.

- Wait until the oil heats up slightly and add to the pan all the plants you just cut beforehand, except the coriander. Then, dirty and pepper to taste.

- Then add the rice to the vegetables' pan and mix everything well. Also, add half of the coconut milk, stir the whole, and pour 4 cups of water.

- To continue, you need to wait until the whole reaches the boiling point (again over medium heat). Then reduce the intensity of the heat a little and let the preparation cook for 15 minutes.

- During these 15 minutes, the rice should never dry completely. If you ever see that this is the case, add more liquid.

- Once the 15 minutes have elapsed, add the shrimp. Also, add the rest of the coconut milk.

- After the 5 minutes have passed, turn off the heat and remove the pan from the heat.

- Then add the chopped coriander, stir the whole and serve.

WHITE RICE

Ingredients

- 1 cup white rice

- 2 cups of water

- One teaspoon salt

- One tablespoon vegetable oil

Preparation

- First, find a medium saucepan in good condition to cook the white rice.

- Then add the white rice, 2 cups of water, salt, and vegetable oil. Basically, add all four ingredients at the same time.

- Then, stir everything only once.

- Place your pan on high heat. Your mixture will begin to boil.

- You will see how the water will dry in a few minutes (maximum five). At this time (the surface of the rice will stop boiling), lower the heat to a minimum and cover the pan. Look at the photo to see the exact moment when to lower the fire. Observe that the water has dried, but there is still moisture and bubbles.

- Ensure to take away the lid from the pan and taste the grain to check the consistency. Rice should be ready. If this is not the case (remember that some kitchens are less powerful), cover the pan again for 5 minutes.

- If the rice is already ready, turn the heat off and remove the pan. This is especially important if your kitchen is electric because the heat could ruin everything.

CHAPTER SEVEN

DAY SEVEN - DAY NINE: EASY DIGESTION

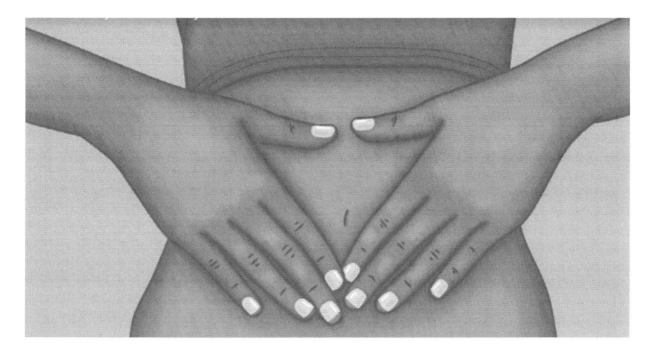

It is important to know that a healthy diet is part of a context of good habits that help the whole body stay healthy and fit to combat poor digestion. Then, it would also be appropriate to keep in mind the importance of greater attention and food awareness. Some general rules should always be kept in mind: eat five meals a day (small and frequent), eat lots of fruit and vegetables, and avoid, or try to limit, fries, chocolate, alcohol, and carbonated drinks. These are all reflux foods, which certainly don't help.

SEAFOOD PAELLA

Ingredients

- 2 cups rice

- 4 cups shrimp broth

- Squid: 15 oz.

- Fresh shrimp: 17 oz.

- Shellfish: 1 cup

- Onion: As required

- Tomatoes: 4 oz.

- ½ cup of red pepper

- Two cloves garlic: 2 oz.

- ½ cup of peas

- Fresh parsley leaves: 5 oz.

- Olive oil: 4 cups

- Salt: As required

134

- A few sprigs of saffron (or yellow dye, otherwise): 2 oz.

Preparation

- First, clean and peel the shrimp. Take the buds and shells to prepare a broth.

- In parallel, it is necessary to clean the squid and cut them into slices.

- Then clean the shells with plenty of water to remove any sand residue.

- Then, take a paella pan or a pan large and deep enough. Heat a little olive oil to sauté the onion, garlic, pepper, and tomato (all previously peeled and cut into small cubes). Add some seasoned ingredients to these ingredients with a little salt and pepper.

- Add the pieces of squid, then the shells. Let them come back for a few minutes. Some ingredients will begin to disgorge water, which will form a kind of broth.

- Then add the 2 cups of rice and mix everything. Then, add 4 cups of shrimp broth that you prepared at the beginning of this recipe (with the buds and shells). If you can't complete four cups, add a little water to get the volume of liquid you want.

- Before adding the saffron strands, or otherwise, a small teaspoon of yellow food coloring, stir everything well. Then, let your mixture boil for 3 minutes.

- To continue, add the fresh peas, shrimp, and parsley. The latter must be finely chiseled.

- Then check the seasoning of the mixture, and correct it with salt and pepper, if necessary.

- Let the paella cook until the liquid evaporates almost completely. At this time, decorate the rice with a few strips of pepper and some shrimp with their shells.

- Then reduce the heat and cover the paella pan.

- Then, let the rice cook for 15 minutes. Once this time has elapsed, taste it. If you are satisfied with the consistency, remove the paella from the heat. Serve your dish, watering the rice with a drizzle of olive oil.

Ingredients

- 17 oz. of zucchini well washed and cut.

- 4 cups vegetable broth

- Chopped Onion: 4 oz.

- Two cloves of garlic (crushed): 2 oz.

- One bouquet of fresh coriander or a bouquet garnished

- Salt and pepper to taste

- Two tablespoons butter

- One teaspoon of olive oil

- One teaspoon of crème fraiche per person

- Chopped parsley: 20 oz.

- Parmesan cheese: 4 oz.

Preparation

- Ensure you put the butter and olive oil in a large saucepan. Add the garlic and onion and cook over medium heat until the onions become transparent.

- Add the sliced zucchini. Cook over medium heat for 4/5 minutes, stirring not to burn the plants.

- Pour the vegetable broth to the point where the zucchini is well covered.

- The next step is to add salt and pepper to taste. Then, you have to mix everything, taste it and adjust the seasoning, if necessary.

- Start cooking zucchini until it becomes tender.

- Then add the coriander. Mix everything, taste it and rectify, if necessary. Remove from heat.

- Move the contents of the pan in a robot or mixer to obtain a cream. If necessary, add more broth or otherwise add water until you get the desired thickness and be careful not to remain too liquid.

- Then turn the zucchini cream into the pan to heat it well. Serve in soup plates or small bowls, adding a spoon of fresh cream to each plate. Decorate with fresh parsley.

- Sprinkle each plate with grated Parmesan cheese.

PUMPKIN SOUP

Ingredients

- 5 cups of vegetable broth

- Onion: 2 oz.

- Pepper: 2 oz.

- One branch of celery: 2 oz.

- A few fresh coriander leaves: 1 oz.

- Pumpkin: 18 oz.

- Salt: As required

- Ground black pepper: As required

Preparation

- First, cut the pumpkin's flesh into pieces of about 2 centimeters. Then, remove seeds and thick skin.

- Then chop the onion and pepper (already washed) into three or four coarse pieces. In the case of onion, it must be peeled beforehand, and in the pepper case, the branch, white parts, and seeds should be removed.

- The celery branch can also be cut into large pieces.

- Then, in a large saucepan, place the pieces of pumpkin, onion, pepper, and the broth of your choice.

- Then heat them until boiling. They should be left to cook until the pumpkin's flesh becomes tender.

- Then you will add the coriander and celery to let the soup cook for another 5 minutes.

- Proceed to add some quantity of salt and pepper to taste.

- Pour all the ingredients and liquid into a food processor or blender, and mix them until you get cream, without lumps.

- Once passed to the blender, you can put the soup back in the pan and continue to heat it over low heat to keep it warm until it is time to serve.

- Once your velvety is served, add a small spoon of butter to the plate, and you can also sprinkle it with grated Parmesan cheese.

Ingredients

- Chopped green beans: 7 oz.

- Cut potatoes: 7 oz.

- Red tomatoes: 5 oz.

- Onion: 2 oz.

- Peppers: As requires

- One tablespoon Garam Masala powder

- One teaspoon ground cinnamon

- One teaspoon turmeric

- Salt: As required

- Olive oil: 2 cups

Preparation

- In a large saucepan, pour olive oil and sauté the potatoes and green beans for 5 minutes, constantly stirring so that the vegetables do not stick.

- Add the onion cut into small cubes, garam masala, cinnamon, and turmeric. Mix everything for a few minutes.

- Then add the peppers cut into cubes, the contents of the half can of tomatoes, a little salt, and pepper. Mix again.

- Let your curry sauce reach the boiling point. You will need to lower the source of heat and cover the pan.

- Continue cooking, stirring occasionally. If you deem it necessary, add 1/4 cup of water so that the liquid does not dry too much.

- Cooking should take about half an hour. It depends on the pieces of potatoes. Try them after this time to validate if they are cooked enough. You can insert the tip of a fork into one of the pieces, and if you can get it out of it easily, they are ready.

- Turn off the heat and leave your curry to rest for 5 minutes. After that, it will be ready to be served.

BAKED SWEET POTATOES

Ingredients

- Two large sweet potatoes: 8 oz.

- Olive oil: 2 cups

- Grated Parmesan cheese: 3 oz.

- Salt: As required

- Garlic powder: As required

- Thyme: As required

- Rosemary: As required

Preparation

- First, preheat the oven to 200c.

- The next step is to peel the sweet potatoes and cut them as if you are preparing fries. Yes, it sticks between half a centimeter and a centimeter thick.

- Then, in a bowl, mix a drizzle of olive oil with a pinch of salt, another pinch of garlic powder, and a few spoons of the grated Parmesan cheese. Also, add your favorite spices in quantities according to your taste.

- Place the sweet potato sticks in the bowl, and mix them with the oil paste, cheese, and spices. Next, add the sweet potatoes or chopped potatoes to the bowl and soak them in the mixture. Make sure the potato pieces are well covered with your homemade condiment.

- Then place the sweet potatoes in an oven-going tray (covered with a sheet of baking paper or aluminum foil). Separate the potatoes: they must not stick and do not remain superimposed.

- Bake the tray for 25 or 35 minutes, or until you get cooked and slightly crispy potatoes. Note that the time for cooking will depend on the power of your oven.

- Once the time has elapsed, take the potatoes out of the oven and let them sit for a few minutes. When serving your sweet potatoes, you can sprinkle them with more grated Parmesan cheese to taste (and without limit).

MASHED POTATO

Ingredients

- Five large potatoes: 30 oz.

- Whole milk: 3.5 oz.

- Butter: 1.5 oz.

- Salt: As required

- Water: 4 cups

Preparation

- First, it is necessary to wash and peel the potatoes. They must remain clean, without shoots or black holes, so that your puree is impeccable.

- Then cut the peeled potatoes into medium-sized pieces.

- Then cook the potatoes in boiling salted water for about 10-15 minutes. You will know that my pieces of potatoes are well cooked when you manage to pierce them with a knife without them disintegrating.

- Heat the milk (or rather cooldown) simultaneously as the potatoes boil.

- After cooking the potatoes, we will crush them. First, you have to drain the pieces. Ensure that you select the method suitable for when you want to crush your potatoes, either a mashed press, a robot or mixer, or the one that is always by hand: a simple fork. We will do this procedure when the potatoes are hot because the heat will allow the ingredients to come together and blend into a delicious mash. With cold potatoes, the results will not be the same.

- After crushing your vegetables for the first time, you will always have large fragments mixed with a kind of applesauce. Don't worry about them. Add the butter cut into small cubes, scattered on this first dough. The immediate effect you will notice is that the heat of the potatoes will melt the butter. So, stir everything and keep crushing your mixture.

- Then, pour a little warm milk over the puree and salt the mixture to your liking. Crush, crush and crush the pieces, again and again, alternating more milk here and there. This is how the large pieces of potato will eventually disappear. Continue to beat vigorously until you get the creamiest consistency possible.

- Once ready, just enjoy this delicious dish.

BAKED FRIES

Ingredients

- Three potatoes: 20 oz.

- Vegetable oil: 2 cups

- Salt: As required

Preparation

- Proceed to preheat the oven to 180 degrees.

- Then it is necessary to peel the potatoes and cut them into slices about one centimeter or one and a half centimeters thick. Then, it is required to cut these slices into sticks about one centimeter thick.

- You need to fill a large saucepan (or large container) with water to continue. You will use it to soak the cut potatoes for about 10 minutes. The goal is to remove some of the natural starch from the potato, to help them remain firm after cooking.

- After the 10 minutes have passed, take out the potatoes, drain them and dry them with a clean cloth.

- Then you have to place the fries in another bowl to water them with a drizzle of oil. They must be mixed so that the oil is distributed everywhere, which will promote the proper cooking of our fries in the oven.

- To continue, take the plate out of the oven and cover it with a sheet of baking paper or aluminum foil. You can also use the oven rack instead of a hob.

- Then, distribute the fries on the plate or rack and ensure they don't overlap.

- Then bake the potatoes for 45 minutes. Ensure that you watch them from time to time to check the color of your fries. They should not become too dark.

- If your oven doesn't have a cooking mode that produces heat from the top and bottom, you'll be forced to open the oven halfway through cooking to turn all the potatoes over. If your oven sends heat from both sides, you won't have to do anything.

- You should have crispy and golden fries at the end of the cooking time. At this time, take them out of the oven and sprinkle with salt to taste.

Ingredients

- Two carrots: 4 oz.

- Two zucchinis: 2 oz.

- Grated mozzarella cheese: 11 oz.

- Two peppers: 3 oz.

- Grated parmesan cheese: 2.5 oz.

- 12 cups of lasagna

- 3/4 cups of homemade tomato sauce

- 12 fresh basil leaves: 15 oz.

- Oregano powder: As required

- Salt: As required

- Ground black pepper: As required

- Olive oil: 2 cups

Preparation

- Put on the oven and preheat it to 180 degrees.

- To continue, you have to peel the carrots and then cut them into thin slices. In the case of peppers, they must be washed and then opened with a knife to remove the seeds and white membranes from their interior. Once done this, cut the skin into julienne.

- Then, find a baking tray, and place the carrot and pepper pieces. Dirty and peppery to taste and sprinkle with olive oil.

- Bring the vegetables to the oven and let them cook for 15 minutes.

- While the vegetables cook, wash the zucchini, wring them out, and cut them into slices, lengthwise.

- Take the tray out 15 minutes later with the carrots and peppers. If there is liquid left at the bottom of the tray, make the necessary movements to make it flow.

- Then add to the tray the slices of zucchini. Salt and pepper the latter and pour a drizzle of olive oil over the whole.

- Put the tray back in the oven for an additional 15 minutes of cooking.

- While the vegetable cooks, grate the mozzarella cheese. Then do the same with Parmesan.

- Then, wash the basil leaves and wring them out.

- When the vegetables' cooking time has passed, take the tray out of the oven.

- Use a large rectangular container to start assembling the lasagna. First, it is necessary to cover the bottom with sheets of dough. Then, cover this with a layer of tomato sauce.

- To continue, place a new layer of dough leaves, and this time, cover it with a layer of cooked vegetables and then another layer of grated mozzarella.

- Then, sprinkle the set of ground oregano and distribute the basil leaves.

- Then repeat the whole procedure until you have finished all the ingredients.

- Finally, add a new layer of grated Parmesan cheese. Use all Parmesan cheese.

- It's time to bake the lasagna for 30 minutes.

- Once the cooking time has elapsed, take the lasagna out of the oven and wait 5 minutes before cutting the first piece.

GRILLED SALMON PAVÉ

Ingredients

- Two pavers of fresh salmon: 20 oz.

- Olive oil: 2 cups

- One lemon: 2 oz.

- Salt: As required

- Black pepper: As required

Preparation

- First, heat a board or a large pan on very high heat. Then, pour a small drizzle of olive oil into it.

- Then, salt and pepper the salmon pavers and cook them in a pan.

- Depending on the pavers' thickness, salmon may take longer to cook. In principle, calculate 2 minutes on each side. After this time has elapsed, you can reduce the temperature of the fire to half and leave it a little more cooking time for the fish. Since salmon is a fatty fish, it will cook in its juices or fat.

- Once the salmon pavers are ready, remove them from the pan or board, and place each on a plate.

- Cut the lemon and express each half on each pavement to sprinkle it with the juice generously.

AVOCADO SALMON TARTARE

Ingredients

- Salmon: 15 oz.

- One ripe avocado: 8 oz.

- One teaspoon soy sauce

- One teaspoon Worcestershire sauce

- One teaspoon mustard

- One teaspoon rice or apple vinegar

- Lemon juice: 2 cups

- One tablespoon caper

- Ground black pepper: As required

- Olive oil: 2 cups

Preparation

- Ensure that the salmon is clean: skinless, thornless. Then, when calculating the amount of salmon listed in the ingredient list, make it with clean salmon.

- The pickles must be already well-cut. First, we will measure the tablespoon with the pickles previously cut. It's the same for chives. It must be well washed and chiseled.

- You will cut the fish into cubes using a good knife. The ideal knife will slice the salmon with a single cut to avoid the risk of crushing or deforming it.

- Then we have to take care of the lawyer. After that, we will cut it into pieces, the same size as the fish.

- Then, we will leave the salmon aside for a little while. This, to prepare a dressing with the liquid Ingredients soy sauce, lemon juice, Worcestershire sauce, vinegar, a drizzle of oil, and mustard.

- Then, mix the salmon with this marinade in a bowl and season it with salt and pepper to taste (the latter ingredient is totally optional).

- To continue, we will pass the container to the refrigerator so that the meat soaks up this juice. It is better to cover the container so that the salmon does not dry.

- We will leave the salmon resting for 20 minutes.

- Once this time has elapsed, we will take the salmon out of the refrigerator and mix it with the chopped pickles, capers (chopped, preferably, but it depends on the cook's taste), avocado, and chives.

- Then, you will have to taste tartare to check the seasoning. Then, if necessary, we will correct it with salt and pepper.

- To serve the tartare, use a circular kitchen mold and arrange it in the form of a timpani on each plate.

CHAPTER EIGHT

DAY TEN - DAY TWELVE: GETTING BETTER

As properly explained in previous chapters, many benefits are attached to eating a healthy diet. Aside from the fact that you will not complicate the situations in your stomach, you will begin to look better and feel complete in every other aspect of your life. Also, consuming a nutritious diet provides several health advantages, including lowering the risk of heart disease, stroke, obesity, and type 2 diabetes. Additionally, it might improve a person's mood and give them additional energy.

ORIGINAL SALAD WITH DATES AND MANDARINS

Ingredients

- Arugula, lettuce, or fresh watercress: 20 oz.

- Tangerines: 5 oz.

- Dates: 3 oz.

- White vinegar: 1.5 oz.

- Mandarin or orange juice, or lemon: 4 oz.

- Olive oil: 2 cups

- Sugar: As required

- Salt: As required

- Pepper: As required

Preparation

- Wash the arugula /lettuce/watercress very well.

- Place it in a large bowl.

- Peel one or two tangerines, removing even the skin (the pulp will be left uncovered). Basically, you're going to swell the tangerine.

- Cut each part in half and remove the seeds.

- Add the pieces of mandarin to the container.

- Cut the dates in half and remove the seeds.

- Add the pieces of dates to the container.

- Prepare a dressing for the seasoning of your original salad. Use a little vinegar, citrus juice (either tangerine, orange, or lemon), a pinch of sugar, salt, pepper, and olive oil.

- Stir the mixture. Add it to the container where the other ingredients are.

- Mix the plants and the dressing, and that's it.

RICE SALAD

Ingredients

- Rice: 15 oz.

- One red pepper: 2 oz.

- One medium zucchini: 5 oz.

- Two sausages: 6 oz.

- One red tomato: 2 oz.

- Olive oil: 3 cups

- Ground pepper: As required

- Salt: As required

Preparation

- The first step is to prepare the rice, which is very easy to do.

- The next step is to heat water in a saucepan and cook sausages.

- Then clean the vegetables: pepper, zucchini, and tomato.

- Then remove the head of the pepper and cut it into three or four large pieces. Next, remove the seeds and white inner parts to cut the large pieces into small cubes.

- After, it will be the turn of the tomato and zucchini. Chop them both until you get small cubes.

- Once the sausages are cooked, they will also have to be cut into cubes.

- Once the rice is cooked, the next thing is to let it cool. Keep in mind that the rice must be well loose. This is the ideal texture to use for a rice salad.

- Finally, take a large bowl to mix the rice with the pieces of vegetables and sausages. Salt and add pepper to taste. Then, mix it all up.

- Top your rice salad with a drizzle of olive oil. That's all; your salad is ready.

Ingredients

- Cooked chickpeas: 15 oz.

- Spinach: 8 oz.

- Pepper: As required

- Salt: As required

- Olive oil: 4 cups

Preparation

- Clean the spinach thoroughly.

- Cut them into elongated pieces.

- Place the pieces in a container. Add the chickpeas (wrung out).

- Sprinkle to your liking.

- Add olive oil according to the amount your body demands

CHICKEN PASTA SALAD

Ingredients

- Macaroni: 5.5 oz.

- One chicken breast

- A few lettuce leaves

- A few leaves of arugula

- ½ cup of onion

- ¼ cup of red pepper

- Peanuts: 4 oz.

- Oregano: As required

- Olive oil: 3 cups

- Salt: As required

- ½ cup of lemon (optional)

Preparation

- You will need to boil the pasta in a saucepan with water and a pinch of salt. After some time, remove them from the heat, use a filter to separate them from the water, and pass them to cold water to stop cooking.

- Grill the chicken breast. Let it sit once ready, and then crumble or cut it into pieces.

- Cut the lettuce and arugula leaves with your hands. Calculate the portions according to your tastes.

- Chop the onion and pepper into small cubes.

- Then simply mix all the ingredients in a salad bowl.

- Add a pinch of salt and another pepper, a touch of oregano, and a drizzle of olive oil.

- Depending on your preference, you can add a little lemon juice.

FATTOUCHE SALAD

Ingredients

- Four cups of lettuce

- Peppermint leaves: 12 oz.

- Three sprigs of parsley: 3 oz.

- Two medium tomatoes: 6 oz.

- A cucumber: 4 oz.

- Two medium radishes: 6 oz.

- A purple onion: 4 oz.

- A lemon: 2 oz.

- Pita bread: 2 oz.

- Three teaspoons of Zaatar (This ingredient can be obtained in any Arabic food store)

- Salt: As required

- Pepper: As required

Preparation

- First, toast the pita bread with a microwave. Then, place it (in pieces) on the glass plate or plate.

- Heat them for a minute. Then, touch them to make sure they are grilled. Otherwise, heat them for another minute until you get a crispy texture. Consider that every microwave is different. In mine, for example, pieces of pita bread take two minutes to become crispy.

- Then cut the vegetables: lettuce into medium pieces, tomatoes, and cucumber into medium cubes (calculate that you can take them with the help of a fork). Onions and radishes should be chopped into julienne.

- Then separate the mint and parsley leaves and cut them into tiny pieces.

- Mix everything together.

- Add the lemon, zaatar, salt, and pepper (to taste).

- Finally, crush the pita bread into pieces, and cover the mixture with this.

- Remix everything and serve the salad.

RABBIT

Ingredients

- Two tablespoons of Dijon mustard

- Rabbit: 30 oz.

- Carrot: 6 oz.

- One white onion

- One green or red pepper

- Two cloves of garlic: 1 oz.

- Two tablespoons of fresh cream

- 5 cups of chicken or vegetable broth

- White wine: 1 cup

- One tablespoon of cornstarch

158

- Two teaspoons of paprika powder

- Two cups of vegetable oil

- Salt: As required

- Ground black pepper: As required

Preparation

- To begin with, it is necessary to cut the rabbit into pieces. I prefer to ask the butcher for cutting, and you can do the same, to save yourself time in the kitchen.

- Then we will take care of the vegetables. First, peel the onion and cut it into small cubes.

- Then it is necessary to peel the garlic and chop it into tiny pieces. Afterward, you have to peel the carrot and cut it into relatively thin slices.

- In the case of pepper, we will remove the rest of the branch, the white parts of the inside. Then we will cut the pulp into julienne.

- For the next step, it is necessary to heat a drop of oil in a large saucepan to brown the rabbit pieces. Again, we will turn them over as they cook to brown the entire surface evenly.

- Once the pieces are golden, we will reserve them in another container. Then we will add a little more oil to the pan to cook the onion and garlic. They should be left to cook for a few minutes until the onion becomes slightly transparent.

- Then it is necessary to add the carrot slices and pepper pieces to the pan. We will let them cook for about 5 minutes.

- It is necessary to place a few spoonfuls of broth in a small cup during this time. We will use them to dissolve flour or cornstarch using a fork. When mixing, all lumps must be removed. Once a uniform paste is obtained, it must be kept aside.

- After five minutes of cooking the vegetables, add the Dijon mustard and the crème Fraiche to the saucepan. Then you have to add a pinch of salt, one pepper, and yet another of paprika. Then, you have to mix everything well.

- We will heat the broth in a large saucepan, adding the cup's contents to dilute the cornstarch. You must mix everything well and let it warm.

- Then, add the vegetables to the broth and a small glass of wine and rabbit pieces.

- Then cover the pan and let the rabbit cook for 20 minutes.

- After this period, it is necessary to taste the sauce. Next, it is required to correct the seasoning with a bit of salt, pepper, paprika, or even a little wine. Then, it is essential to check that the rabbit's meat is tender enough (If this is not the case, we can let the rabbit cook for a few more minutes.

- That's all. Our rabbit with mustard is ready.

CHINESE RAVIOLI OR GYOZAS

Ingredients

- Prepared Chinese ravioli dough: 8 oz.

- Ground pork: 7 oz.

- One egg: 2 oz.

- A teaspoon of cornstarch or Maïzena

- A branch of chives or Chinese cabbage: 4 oz.

- Light soy sauce: 3 cups

- Sesame oil: 4 cups

Preparation

- First, wash the branch of chives or Chinese cabbage well. Then, drain it, remove the root remains, and chisel it.

- Then place the minced pork in a medium bowl and add the egg, chives, or Chinese cabbage, a little soy sauce, cornstarch, and a few drops of sesame oil. Mix everything and let this stuffing sit for an hour in the refrigerator. Ensure that you close it with a cloth or plastic film.

- After this time has elapsed, place a spoon of stuffing in the center of each sheet of gyoza dough. Then, join the edges of the dough.

- Repeat this process with all the sheets of ravioli dough until you finish the stuffing.

- Then we will start cooking gyozas. First, take a large saucepan and boil enough water to cook all Chinese ravioli.

- Place the Chinese ravioli in hot water and let them cook for about 10-15 minutes or until they start floating. Then, remove the gyozas and drain them.

- Then take another large pot or pan and heat a drizzle of vegetable oil. You need to choose a pot or pan with enough room for ravioli.

- Once the oil is hot, cook the gyozas for a few minutes. The goal is to brown them slightly and that they take on the characteristic texture of the dish. They must remain a little crispy on one side but soft on the other.

- That's all. Serve the Chinese ravioli immediately, accompanied by a little soy sauce in a small container.

CHAPTER NINE

DAY THIRTEEN - DAY FIFTEEN: FOOD AS MEDICINE

You must consume your food as medicine to not end up consuming medicine as food. Research has shown that most people who take their meals very seriously rarely fall sick because of their increased immunity from the food materials they consume. At the same time, those who rarely eat are prone to several illnesses due to their weak immune system and absence of nutrients.

STUFFED ZUCCHINI

Ingredients

- Two large round or elongated zucchini: 30 oz.

- Minced meat: 11 oz.

- Two Medium onion

- One small tomato

- One clove garlic: 0.5 oz.

- ½ cup of red pepper

- Grated Gruyère cheese: 2 oz.

- Grated Parmesan cheese: 2 oz.

- Oregano: 1 oz.

- Cumin: 3 oz.

- Olive oil: 2 cups

- Salt: As required

Preparation

- Chop the zucchini in half lengthwise if they are elongated. If it is round zucchini, instead remove some "lid" in the upper part of each piece to create a resemblance to a small saucepan or container.

- With a knife, make several deep cuts in each half of the zucchini when it comes to elongated zucchini. In the case of round zucchini, do this procedure only for the bottom part.

- Make cuts in the direction of magnitude and length. Make sure the knife does not penetrate to the bottom as it could break the zucchini.

- Once the cuts are made, using a fork, remove the inner pulp from each of the zucchini halves for the elongated ones, and from the largest part, in the case of round zucchini. Ideally, you should remove about 2/3 of the pulp from the vegetable. Once removed, reserve it.

- Chop the half onion, tomato, pepper, and garlic into small cubes. I also take the pulp of the zucchini to cut it in the same way as the other ingredients.

- Then sauté the garlic, onion, pepper, tomato, and zucchini pulp.

- Add the ground pork. Mix everything together.

- Then add a little oregano, cumin, salt, and pepper.

- Reduce the heat and let everything cook for 20 minutes. If the mixture becomes very dry, pour a 1/2 cup of water.

- Once the time has elapsed, taste the mixture to check the seasoning. Add more salt and pepper, if necessary. It would help if you were careful that the mixture does not become too dry. But on the other side, you're not going to make soup either.

- Then place the zucchini halves in the oven, 180 degrees for 10 minutes, to cook them a little.

- After these 10 minutes, take out the zucchini but leave the oven on.

- Once the stuffing is ready, you can start placing it in each zucchini: simply place a spoon of minced meat on each half of the zucchini, then add a little grated cheese and sprinkle everything with Parmesan cheese.

- Bring the zucchini back to the oven, this time raising the temperature to 200 degrees. Use the same tray as before.

- Ensure that it cooks to the point where they become golden brown.

AVOCADO SALAD

Ingredients

- A large red tomato: 5 oz.

- A white radish: 4 oz.

- A white or red onion: 6 oz.

- Olive oil: 4 cups

- Lemon juice: 3 cups

- Freshly ground black pepper: As required

- Salt: As required

Preparation

- First, cut the onion into halves. Then, take one of the halves by cutting the onion into ribbons.

- Then wash the radish and cut it.

- In the case of tomatoes, wash them and cut them into slices as thin as possible.

- Then, cut the avocado into halves and remove the core with a hillside. To continue, remove the skin and cut each half into thin slices.

- Then water the avocado with the juice of the lemon to prevent it from blackening. This blackening results from the oxidation of the avocado once its pulp has come into contact with air.

- You have to find a beautiful tray to serve the salad to continue. You can arrange the vegetables as you like. However, the excellent idea is to alternate the slices of avocado, tomato, and radish.

- Once these three vegetables are arranged on the tray, decorate them with the onion pieces and sprinkle with a little more lemon juice.

- Finally, salt and pepper to taste, and top with a drizzle of olive oil, very fine.

BAKED EGGPLANT

Ingredients

- Sliced mozzarella cheese: 4 oz.

- One small white onion: 2 oz.

- One red pepper: 1 oz.

- Ground black pepper: As required

- Salt: As required

- Two large cloves of garlic: 1 oz.

- Ground beef: 9 oz.

- Two large purple eggplants: 4 oz.

- Grated parmesan cheese: 1.5 oz.

- Bay leaves: 4 oz.

- Vegetable oil: 3 cups

- Sunflower: 2 oz.

- Rapeseed: 3 oz.

- Corn: 3 oz.

- One teaspoon of oregano powder

- 1/2 teaspoon rosemary coffee

Preparation

- Increase the heat of the oven to 180 degrees.

- While we wait for it to warm up, we will prepare the eggplants. First, we must wash them because we will not remove the skin. On the other hand, they must be cut in halves, lengthwise.

- Once the eggplants are in halves, we will make cross or grid shapes on the pulp in the center of each half, using a sharp knife. We will do this in the same way as our other stuffed zucchini recipe.

- Then it is necessary to fill a large container with water to soak the pieces of eggplant for about 10 minutes.

- During this time, we can begin to prepare the farce. First, peel the onion and cut it into small cubes.

- We will also peel the garlic cloves, cut them very finely, or crush them.

- Then it is necessary to wash the red pepper. Then we will remove the seeds, the internal white parts, and the remains of the stem to finally cut the flesh into small cubes.

- Once the 10 minutes of soaking have passed, we will take the eggplants out of the water and drain them very well.

- Then, you have to arrange each half of the eggplant on a container or dish going to the oven and cover them with a drizzle of oil in the shape of an S, which will form many curves on the pulp of each.

- Then we will bake the eggplants for 20 minutes.

- During this time, we will continue the preparation of the farce. First, it is necessary to heat a pan with a tablespoon of oil, then cook the garlic and onion pieces over medium heat until a slightly transparent color is obtained.

- Then it is necessary to incorporate the pieces of red pepper and minced meat. After mixing everything, let it cook for 12 to 15 minutes, stirring frequently.

- Once the cooking time of the eggplants has elapsed, we will take them out of the oven.

- The preliminary cuts dug in the center of the flesh will help us remove the center of each half with the help of a spoon. Leave only the flesh closest to the skin, and above all, be careful not to damage it. This way, we will get a kind of "container" to fill.

- Then it is necessary to chop the removed flesh. Then, it must be mixed with the rest of the stuffing.

- It's time to season the stuffing with rosemary, oregano, as well as salt and pepper to taste. Then, you have to mix everything well.

- After 15 minutes of cooking the stuffing, turn off the heat and start stuffing the eggplant halves using a ladle or kitchen spoon. Distribute the stuffing to Templar each half of the eggplant.

- Then we will distribute the slices of mozzarella to cover each half, and we will top them with the grated cheese, distributed in equal parts. Finally, place a whole or lump bay leaf on each half.

- Bake the eggplants again, to gratin them. Ensure that the oven is heated to 200 degrees centigrade and let them cook for 10 minutes (or 15 minutes, if necessary, to melt the cheese well).

- It's ready. Once the baking time has passed, you can take out the eggplants stuffed with minced meat to eat.

Ingredients

- Béchamel sauce: 16 oz.

- Minced lamb or veal beef: 17 oz.

- One white onion: 2 oz.

- Three cloves garlic: 2 oz.

- Three purple eggplants: 4 oz.

- Three red tomatoes: 4 oz.

- Grated yellow cheese: 8.5 oz.

- A cup of dry white wine

- Two potatoes: 4 oz.

- Salt: As required

- Black or white pepper powder: 4 oz.

- Vegetable oil: 3 cups

- Herbs: As required

- Cumin: 2 oz.

- Paprika powder: 4 oz.

Preparation

- First, it is necessary to wash the eggplants well. Then we will cut them into slices one centimeter thick.

- Then we will soak them in water using a suitable sized container. Finally, we will rest them for 30 minutes to remove the bitter taste of this ingredient.

- Then, peel and cut the onions and garlic. In the former case, we will cut them into small cubes. For the second, it must be cut into small pieces or crushed. Then we will reserve both ingredients.

- To continue, it is necessary to grate the tomatoes (already clean). We will also book them.

- Then it is necessary to peel the potatoes and cut them into slices about one finger thick.

- It's time to fry the garlic and onion in a hot pan, with plenty of oil.

- When the onion becomes transparent, add the minced meat and let it cook until it gets a slightly golden color. It is essential to mix it constantly so that it cooks evenly.

- When the meat is a little golden, we will incorporate the tomato. You will have to let it cook for 5 minutes, then add the wine and spices: a pinch of salt, a touch of pepper to taste, and the same for paprika, cumin, and herbs of Provence. Spice lovers can increase the amount of cumin and paprika (maximum one teaspoon).

- Mix everything well and cook for another 15 to 20 minutes. The purpose is to evaporate all the liquid released by tomatoes and meat. Therefore, it is important to monitor cooking, stir ingredients frequently, and, if necessary, reduce the intensity of the fire.

- At this moment, we will preheat the oven to 180 degrees.

- Then we will collect the eggplant slices, drain them, dry them and cook them in another saucepan with a bit of oil. Each slice should be cooked on both sides until a slightly golden color is obtained. At that time, take them out of the oil and drain them.

- Then, it is also necessary to fry the potato slices until you get a beautiful golden color, on two sides, for each slice.

- With eggplants, potatoes, and meat already cooked, we can move on to the next step of the recipe. In the case of meat, I recommend that you taste it to check the seasoning and, if necessary, correct it with salt or other spices.

- To continue, we will arrange the potato slices at the bottom of a container going to the oven to form the first layer. Then, it will be necessary to deposit the meat and eggplants in alternating layers as if they were lasagna. First, we will arrange a layer of eggplant on the potatoes, a layer of meat, and another layer of eggplant until the ingredients are finished. In principle, we will have enough material to make at least two layers of eggplant and two layers of cooked meat.

- Then we will dip our layers in the béchamel sauce.

- To finish the preparation, we must create the last layer of grated cheese to gratin our moussaka.

- This is the time to bake the moussaka for about 20 minutes or until the cheese melts.

BAKED LAMB

Ingredients

- Lamb chops: 21 oz.

- Two cloves garlic: 1 oz.

- White onion: 6 oz.

- Potatoes: 9 oz.

- One cup of dry white wine or red wine

- Vegetable oil: 3 cups

- Fresh rosemary: 4 oz.

- Oregano powder: 5 oz.

- Fresh parsley: 3 oz.

- Salt: As required

Preparation

- Preheat the oven to 200 degrees.

- Then you have to peel the garlic cloves and chop them very finely.

- Then, in the case of the onion, it must be peeled, removed, and then cut into slices or cubes. If you cut it into slices, separate the circles inside each slice to get raw onion rings.

- To continue, it is necessary to prepare the potatoes. First, you have to choose whether you want to peel them or not. If not, wash them very well. Then cut them into quarters.

- This is the time also to prepare parsley. But, first, it must be washed well, drained, and finally, chisel the leaves.

- To continue, we will need an oven-safe container with enough places to hold the chops. Preferably, use a Pyrex-type container or a casserole resistant to high temperatures.

- So, pour a drizzle of oil into the oven-safe container, and add the chopped garlic. Also, pour a teaspoon of powdered oregano and a few sprigs of rosemary. Then, mix the whole.

- Then place the lamb chops in the container and soak them in the mixture. Do the same with potato pieces. If you wish, you can help yourself with a kitchen brush to make sure you cover the entire surface of each chop and potato with a mixture of oil and seasonings.

- To continue, place the pieces of onion on the chops, pour the wine into the container and cover everything with a last drizzle of oil, rather discreet but well distributed over the whole.

- This is the time to bring the chops to the oven, to let them cook for 30 minutes. Once the first 15 minutes have passed, you will need to return to the oven to rotate the chops and potatoes. In this way, they will cook on the other side for the tenth half of the cooking time. At this time, you will also need to water them with the cooking juice.

- Once the cooking time has passed, please take out the lamb ribs and serve them as soon as possible.

Ingredients

- Lamb: 17 oz.

- Salt: As required

- Ground pepper: As required

- Four cloves garlic: 3 oz.

- Two small white onions: 4 oz.

- Herbs

- A cup of dry white wine

- Vegetable oil: 4 cups

Preparation

- You need to remove the tray out of the oven to cook lamb. It must be clean and dry.

- Increase the oven to 180 degrees Celsius.

- To continue, peel the garlic cloves and crush them. You can also cut them very finely into pieces as small as possible if you prefer.

- In the case of onions, peel them and cut them into thin slices.

- Then, grease the surface of the oven tray before it is used for cooking.

- Then place the clean piece of meat on the tray and season it with salt and pepper to taste.

- Then pour a drizzle of oil over the meat, only to start massaging it with your fingertips. Do this until you distribute the oil over the entire meat piece's surface.

- To continue, rub the meat's skin with garlic until it distributes throughout the surface, more or less evenly. To distribute it, it is still necessary to massage the meat to mix with the oil of the first layer.

- Then, distribute the onion rings over the piece of lamb and sprinkle with a spoon of herbs of Provence.

- Right after, pour the wine over the lamb and its onions.

- Baking lamb shoulder in the oven

- To continue, bake the lamb and let it cook for 60 minutes for a one-kilo lamb or 90 minutes for a one-and-a-half-kilo lamb.

- When half the cooking time has passed, consider returning to the oven stinks of turning the meat. It will also be necessary to water it with the cooking juice, pouring it on the lamb. If it seems to you that you do not have enough liquid, you can add a little water.

- Once the cooking time has elapsed, return to the oven to increase the oven temperature to 220 degrees. Then, turn the piece of lamb over again for even cooking, and drizzle it again with the cooking juice to avoid drying out. Furthermore, if you need liquid, you can add a little water.

- Let the lamb cook for another 20 minutes so that the skin becomes golden and a little crispy. Tip: After the first 10 minutes, turn the meat over again and water it another time.

- That's all. After the last 20 minutes of cooking, your lamb will be ready to take out of the oven, cut it and serve.

CHAPTER TEN

DAY SIXTEEN - DAY SEVENTEEN: BALANCE DIET

A balanced diet satisfies all your nutritional demands. Humans require a specific quantity of calories and nutrients to keep healthy. A balanced diet includes all the nutrients for a gastroparesis patient without going over the recommended daily calorie intake. By eating a balanced diet, individuals may acquire the nutrients and calories they need and avoid consuming junk food or food without nutritional value.

BREAKFAST

HOMEMADE BURRITOS RECIPE

Ingredients

- wheat tortillas: 10 oz.

- A white onion: 3 oz.

- Ground beef: 8 oz.

- Refried bean puree: 3.5 oz.

- Red pepper: 2 oz.

- A green pepper: 2 oz.

- Jalapenos peppers: 2 oz.

- A large red tomato

- Melting cheese (for example, cheddar or grated cheddar): 4 oz.

- A clove of garlic: 0.5 oz.

- Ground black pepper: 2 oz.

- Vegetable oil (rapeseed, corn, or sunflower): 4 cups

Preparation

- First, peel the onion and garlic. Cut the first into small cubes and crush the second.

- Then wash the peppers, tomatoes, and peppers. Remove the inner white part and the seeds of peppers and peppers. Cut everything into small cubes.

- Put the pan in a heat source and add two tablespoons of oil. Add the onion and garlic to cook them over medium heat. The goal is that the onion begins to become a little transparent.

- To continue, add the chopped tomatoes, peppers, and peppers to the mixture. Ensure that it cooks for a few minutes so that the liquid from the tomato evaporates.

- The next step is to remove the ingredients from the pan and set them aside. Then, use the same pan to add the meat. Mix it and lower the intensity of the fire a little.

- Then, let the meat cook in the pan for 15 minutes (or even a little less, depending on the power of your stove).

- You can take advantage of the cooking time of the meat to grate the cheese or cut it.

- Once the meat is cooked, salt and pepper it to taste. Add the ingredients removed before and mix everything.

- Taste the stuffing and correct the seasoning, if necessary.

- Now is the time to prepare the tortillas. It will be necessary to heat (slightly) each tortilla on a board or stove on low heat. It is recommended to grease the surface a little not to stick and blacken the tortillas. You need to perform this step quickly enough not to harden the tortillas.

- Spread each tortilla on a plate and spread a little bean puree on its center. Then cover it with a handful of meat and sprinkle with a good amount of cheese.

- Then fold the ends of the tortilla inwards and roll it up to form a tube.

SALMOREJO

Ingredients

- Ripe tomatoes: 17 oz.

- Olive oil: 4 cups

- One clove of garlic: 0.5 oz.

- Bread: 3.5 oz.

- Boiled egg: 3 oz.

- Iberian ham: 1.5 oz.

- Salt: As required

Preparation

- First, it is necessary to crumble the bread from the day before.

- Then boil water and cook the tomatoes for 2 minutes. Then drain them and soak them in cold water. In this way, you will be able to remove the skin of each fruit very easily.

- To continue, crush the tomatoes with a fork and mix them with the crumbled bread. Be sure to mix them very well, as the bread must remain well soaked.

- Add a little salt to this mixture. This will contribute to the soaking of the bread with the juices of the tomato. Then, let everything sit for 30 minutes.

- Once this time has passed, the bread should be pretty tender. Then pour the mixture into a food processor or blender.

- To continue, add the peeled garlic clove and olive oil to the blender or robot, along with the bread. If you want the garlic to bring a less strong taste, degerm it before using it.

- Ensure to mix it all up very well until it forms a paste.

- After obtaining a creamy, almost liquid paste, pass it through a sieve to become thinner. This process takes a little time, as the basic mixture is quite thick, so stay patient.

- After filtering your liquid, taste it to check the seasoning. If necessary, correct it with a little more salt and remix everything.

- Then, bring the salmorejo to the refrigerator for 30 minutes.

- Take advantage of the soup's rest time to cook a hard-boiled egg. Once ready, remove the crust and cut it into small cubes.

- Then cut the ham into small cubes, too.

- After 30 minutes have passed, take the salmorejo out of the refrigerator. Serve on hollow plates and garnish each serving with cooked egg and ham pieces. Decorate with a drizzle of olive oil.

LUNCH

SPANISH CHICKPEA SOUP

Ingredients

- Dry chickpeas: 11 oz.

- Chorizos: 5 oz.

- Bacon: 1 oz.

- Three Potatoes: 8 oz.

- Two carrots: 4 oz.

- Pepper: As required

- Onion: As required

- Two cloves garlic: 1 oz.

- Two bay leaves: 5 oz.

- One tablespoon paprika

- Salt: As required

- Olive oil: 2 cups

Preparation

- The day before preparing your recipe, soak the chickpeas in a large saucepan with water. They should stay in the water for 12 hours.

- Chop the peeled onion, peeled garlic cloves, and pepper into small cubes.

- Chop peeled carrots, tomatoes, and potatoes into medium pieces.

- Cut the bacon or bacon into cubes, not exceeding 1 cm. Chorizos can be cut into pieces of 2 or 3 cm.

- Wash and drain the chickpeas soaked the day before and place them in a saucepan with 2 liters of water. Cook them over medium heat.

- Take advantage of the cooking time of chickpeas to sauté onion, garlic, pepper, and tomatoes over low heat for 10 minutes. Book them.

- Ensure you add the chorizo and bacon to the chickpeas after 30 mins and let them cook for another 10 minutes.

- Add the cooked vegetable mixture to the chickpeas. Also, add bay leaves, paprika powder, a little salt, and a little pepper.

- That's all. You can serve your chickpea soup in the Spanish way.

CASTILIAN GARLIC SOUP

Ingredients

- 4 cups of water or vegetable broth

- Eight cloves of garlic: 3 oz.

- Two eggs: 6 oz.

- Chorizo: 3 oz.

- Bread: 4 oz.

- One teaspoon paprika powder

- Salt: As required

- Olive oil: 3 cups

- Ground pepper: As required

Preparation

- Peel the garlic cloves and cut them very finely

- The next step is to cut the chorizo into thin slices and cut each in half. If you use ham instead, cut it into cubes.

- Cut or crumble the bread into small pieces.

- Crush the eggs in a bowl and beat them.

- Then heat a deep saucepan with a drizzle of olive oil over low heat. Use your usual pot to make soups.

- After the oil has been warmed, add the pieces of garlic and sauté them for 3 minutes, stirring frequently. It should not burn or turn brown.

- To continue, add the pieces of chorizo or ham to the pan.

- Cook the whole thing for another 2 minutes and then add the liquid. Also, add a pinch of salt and another pepper. Mix everything well, wait for the soup to start boiling, and let it cook for 5 minutes.

- Then add the pieces of bread and the two eggs, previously beaten. Mix everything well and taste the soup to check the seasoning. Grind it with a little more salt or pepper, if necessary. Remix everything.

- Remove the soup from the heat and serve right away. Sprinkle each plate with a bit of paprika powder.

Ingredients

- Chicken neck and breasts: 5 oz.

- Water: 6 oz.

- Potatoes: 4 oz.

- Carrot: 2 oz.

- Pumpkin: 4 oz.

- Chives: 3 oz.

- A medium onion: 2 oz.

- Some mint leaves: 1.3 oz.

- Pepper: As required

- A leek: 3 oz.

- A few fresh coriander leaves: 1 oz.

- A few leaves of fresh parsley

- Powdered oregano: 1 oz.

- A bay leaf: 5 oz.

- A branch of celery

- Salt: As required

- Ground pepper: As required

- Soup noodles: 4 oz.

Preparation

- First, it is necessary to heat 2 liters of water in a large saucepan with the chicken pieces. They should be cooked for 15 minutes (once the water is hot). Meanwhile, monitor cooking to remove the foam from the water's surface with a spoon.

- When the chicken is cooking, peel the onion and cut it into julienne. Wash the pepper well, dry it, remove the branch, remove the seeds, and then cut it into julienne. Add these vegetables to the pan.

- Then wash and wring out the leek, remove the root, and cut the rest into slices. Also, add it to the chicken.

- Then add a pinch of salt, another pepper, the oregano leaf, and a bit of oregano to the pan. Increase the spice to suit your preference.

- To continue, remove the skin from the pumpkin and cut it into pieces. Be sure to add it to the pan only after the liquid has boiled.

- Then peel the carrot and cut it into pieces of the same size as the pumpkin. Add them to the pan as well.

- You can proceed to peel the potatoes and cut them into cubes. Then, finally, add them to the pan.

- Let the soup cook again for up to 35 minutes. Meanwhile, wash the aromatic herbs, and chop them finely.

- Once the cooking time has elapsed, taste the broth and, if necessary, correct the seasoning with more salt or pepper. If so, remix the soup.

- Then, add the finely chopped aromatic herbs: coriander, parsley, celery, mint, and chives.

- Let the soup cook for another 5 minutes. Then turn it off and wait 5 minutes of rest before serving your soup.

- If you want to add noodles to your chicken soup, they should be cooked separately, in another saucepan, with a little water. Then, add them to the chicken soup at the time of serving.

CHAPTER ELEVEN

DAY EIGHTEEN: FOOD FOR LIFE

Food is an essential material for life, and that is why you need to consume it regularly. In this chapter, you shall be exposed to several foods to eat that are necessary for your health as a gastroparesis patient.

VEGETABLE BROTH

Ingredients

- Large white onions: 35 oz.

- Celery with its leaves: 35 oz.

- Carrots: 17 oz.

- Three cloves garlic: 1 oz.

- A white leek: 2 oz.

- Branches of coriander: 4 oz.

- Three bay leaves: 4 oz.

Preparation

- First, clean and cut the vegetables into cubes, irregular pieces, slices, or as you wish. There is no rule here.

- Then place all the ingredients in a saucepan with 3 liters of water. Set the temperature to the maximum to boil the water.

- Then, when the water starts to boil, reduce the heat and let the ingredients cook so that the water evaporates. Wait for the water to decrease to half its level. This should take about 45 minutes, depending on your kitchen.

- After this time, use a filter or Chinese to strain the broth, let it cool and place it in containers with lids to preserve it.

LUNCH

COCONUT MILK SOUP

Ingredients

- Stalk of lemongrass (the white part or root): 6 oz.

- A piece of fresh galangal or ginger root: 2 oz.

- Red Thai pepper: 2 oz.

- Fresh coriander: 3 oz.

- Coconut milk: 14 oz.

- Skinless chicken breast: 5 oz.

- $1^{1}/_{2}$ cup chicken broth

- 2 cups of mushrooms of porcini mushrooms or oyster mushrooms

- A tablespoon of lemon juice

- Four lemons: 3 oz.

Preparation

- To begin with, the mushrooms must be well washed and drained. Then, if you haven't cut them yet, now is the time to get to work. Be sure to measure the 2 cups once the mushrooms are already cut.

- Regarding the chicken, it must already be clean and skinless. Then you can cut it into cubes. Do the same if you use turkey. If you use shrimp instead, they should be shelled and clean.

- Then it is necessary to wash the pepper, drain it and open it with a knife to remove the seeds. Then it must be cut into tiny pieces.

- It is necessary to remove the root base from me as the skin regarding lemongrass. Then cut it lengthwise into thin strips.

- Regarding coriander, it must be washed very well, drained and chiseled leaves, to then reserve them.

- Then, peel the piece of galangal or ginger.

- In the case of lemons, cut them into halves.

- To continue, heat a saucepan with 1 1/2 cups of broth.

- Immediately the broth boils, add coconut milk, lemongrass, galangal, ginger, and chili.

- Cover the pan and let the whole infuse for 5 minutes over medium heat.

- After this time has elapsed, remove the lid there and add to the pan the mushrooms, lemon juice, the rest of the broth, and the chicken (or other proteins, if this is the case). Mix everything together.

- Cook to the point where the chicken is well cooked.

- At this point, turn off the heat and sprinkle with chopped coriander to taste.

- Serve each dish of soup accompanied by half a lemon so that each guest can season their soup to taste.

TUNA TATAKI

Ingredients

- Bluefin tuna back fillet: 12 oz.

- Sesame seeds: 2 oz.

- One tablespoon grated fresh ginger

- Soy sauce: 1 oz.

- Mirin rice: 3 oz.

- One tablespoon sesame oil

- One tablespoon of sugar

- One teaspoon optional mustard

Preparation

- To begin with, we will heat in a small saucepan the rice vinegar or mirin, soy sauce, and sugar. Then, we will stir everything well so that the ingredients mix well.

- If you haven't readied your grated ginger yet, start peeling the piece of ginger. Then grate it until you get the equivalent of a tablespoon.

- Then, remove the liquid from the heat and add the spoon of grated ginger. Then also add the sesame oil and mustard. If you don't like sesame oil, you can replace it with a drizzle of olive oil or peanut oil.

- Mix everything well.

- Marinate your piece of tuna in this marinade sauce for an hour

- Next, marinate the tuna in a container in the refrigerator. Use a lid to prevent drying out. Suppose the liquid does not entirely cover the fish; turn it over half the marinade time.

- After marinating the tuna steak, quickly mark it in a pan or board. I recommend passing an oiled paper towel over the cooking surface to prevent the tuna from sticking. The plate should be very hot when depositing the tuna, and we will only mark it lightly on each side. Make sure to cook for a few seconds on each side to get a half-cooked tuna: either cooked outside but raw on the inside.

- After marking the tuna, it will be necessary to pass it on a plate full of sesame grains to cover it with them. Next, you can soak the tuna in what is left of the marinade so that the sesame grains stick faster during contact.

- Cut the tuna into thin slices once your sesame layer is ready, using a large, sharp knife.

- Serve the tuna tataki with everything left of the marinade and juice on the board. This dish is to be consumed cold or at room temperature.

CHAPTER TWELVE

DAY NINETEEN: AVOID STOMACH ISSUES

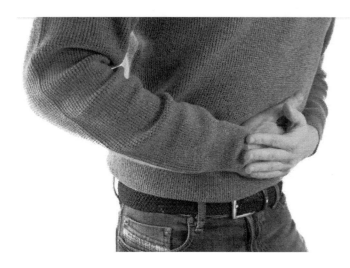

Some people handle their bodies as if they were Ferraris; others as if they were clunkers. A Ferrari body is fed a balanced diet of carbs, lipids, proteins, water, salts, vitamins, and soluble and insoluble fiber — all of which are necessary for indigestion prevention. In this chapter, you shall be exposed to a particular food that is healthy to your guts.

SPAGHETTI WITH CARBONARA

Ingredients

- Four eggs: 10 oz.

- Grated parmesan cheese: 3.5 oz.

- Bacon: 4 oz.

- Olive oil: 4 cups

- Salt: As required

- Pepper powder: 1.5 oz.

- Spaghetti: 8 oz.

Preparation

- First, you have to cut the bacon into strips and fry with medium heat, with olive oil. Let it brown, and then remove from the heat and set aside.

- Then, mix the eggs with the grated Parmesan cheese in a deep bowl until you get a creamy consistency. Add a touch of salt and ground pepper, mix again, and set aside.

- Then you have to cook the pasta. The ideal is to use spaghetti. First, boil a good amount of water. Then, pour the pasta into boiling water with a handful of salt and let it cook for 10 to 12 minutes. Validate the cooking according to your taste by tasting some of the pasta.

- Then, drain them in a large strainer.

- Immediately, the pasta is ready; place it in a large saucepan with the mixture of eggs and cheese. Add the bacon as well. The warmth of the recently cooked pasta will be enough to "lightly cook" the eggs of the carbonara sauce and create the classic consistency of this recipe.

LUNCH

FISH RECIPE IN WHITE WINE SAUCE

Ingredients

- Two cloves of garlic: 1 oz.

- Fresh parsley leaves: 4 oz.

- A medium onion: 5 oz.

- Olive oil: 2 cups

- Salt: As required

- 1/2 cup white wine

- Freshly ground black pepper: 2 oz.

- Two fillets of white fish: 15 oz.

- Two teaspoons of wheat flour

Preparation

- Mix the parsley, onion, garlic, salt, and pepper in a food processor.

- Pour this mixture into a saucepan and heat it over medium heat.

- After 10 minutes of cooking (stirring occasionally), add the white wine and mix it.

- Cook the white wine sauce for another 10 minutes, stirring occasionally.

- Once the time has elapsed, taste it, and add more salt, if necessary.

- Salt and pepper the fish fillets, already clean.

- Place the flour on a plain plate. Place the fish in the flour to cover each side of each fillet well.

- Add oil to a pan and fry the fillets.

- Once cooked, serve the fish fillets covered with the white wine sauce, prepared beforehand.

CHINESE NOODLES WITH VEGETABLES

Ingredients

- Chinese noodles: 8 oz.

- One medium onion: 2 oz.

- Soybean sprouts: 3 oz.

- One clove of garlic: 0.5 oz.

- Two teaspoons of light soy sauce

- 1/2 cup of lemon juice

- 1/4 cup chicken or vegetable broth

- A pinch of sugar

- Salt: As required

- Cayenne pepper powder: 1.5 oz.

- Sesame oil: 0.5 oz.

- A stalk of chives

- 1/2 cup cashew nuts

- Fresh coriander leaves: 3 oz.

Preparation

- First, it is necessary to wash the chives well. Then, drain it and cut it into small slices. Finally, reserve it in a bowl.

- To continue, heat a saucepan with water (at least up to half).

- Then cook the Chinese noodles in hot water, for 5 minutes or until you get an al dente consistency. Then drain them and reserve them.

- To continue, peel the onion and cut it into julienne.

- In the case of the garlic clove, peel it and cut it into very small pieces.

- Then, heat the wok or pan over medium heat with a slight drizzle of oil. Add the cut onion, garlic, and soybean sprouts.

- Then add the soy sauce, the juice of the half lemon, and the chicken broth. Also, add the sugar, a pinch of salt, and another spicy powder.

- Stir everything and let it cook for a few minutes. Then, add the Chinese noodles to the sauce and sauté them over medium heat for a few more minutes.

- Then serve the noodles on a plate.

- To continue, heat another pan with a drizzle of sesame oil, and sauté the white slices of chives until you get a slightly golden color.

- Then add the cashews and sauté them with the chives for two minutes to make them take a little color (without letting them burn).

- Then, place this mixture on the Chinese noodles.

- Finally, sprinkle the dish with green slices of chives and a few fresh coriander leaves.

CHAPTER THIRTEEN

DAY TWENTY: EATING WITHOUT WORRIES

Most people eat their meal with several worries and pains. But as a gastroparesis patient, you should eat your meal like a king or queen. This mentality will be very vital to help your psychology. That is why you need to prepare spicy food containing the appropriate nutrients to serve your body right.

BREAKFAST

FISH BROTH

Ingredients

- fish bones: 15 oz.

- One large onion: 8 oz.

- Two carrots: 4 oz.

- One white leek: 2 oz.

- One sprig of celery: 1.5 oz.

- A cup of dry white wine

Preparation

- First, wash the fish pieces thoroughly to remove impurities, blood, and scales.

- Then cut all the vegetables (previously washed or peeled) into small pieces.

- Then, place all the ingredients in the pan and add 4 liters of water.

- To continue, turn on the fire and let your preparation heat up to a boil. From that moment on, allow 30 minutes of cooking.

- During cooking, a layer of foam and residue will appear on the surface of the liquid. Remove it with a spoon.

- Once time has passed, remove the pan from the heat. Then strain the broth. You can use a coffee filter to make the broth as pure as possible.

- That's all. You can separate it into different containers to store it or even freeze it to keep it longer.

SAUTÉED CHINESE NOODLES

Ingredients

- Chinese rice noodles: 10 oz.

- Beef or veal: 5 oz.

- One red pepper: 1 oz.

- One green pepper: 1 oz.

- One medium onion: 3 oz.

- One medium carrot: 2 oz.

- Two cloves garlic: 1 oz.

- Two tablespoons of soy sauce

- Fresh coriander leaves: 1.5 oz.

- Vegetable oil: 1 cup

Preparation

- First, wash the vegetables and drain them.

- Then you have to cut the vegetables into thin strips. In the case of onion, carrot, and garlic cloves, they must be peeled first. In the case of peppers, the seeds and the inner white part should be removed.

- Your meat must already be clean and defatted. Then it will have to be cut into strips, as you did with vegetables, but a little less fine.

- In the case of parsley, it should be washed and drained. Then it is necessary to separate the leaves and chisel them with a sharp knife. For now, reserve this ingredient.

- Then, you have to heat a saucepan with water. Use the hot water to soak the noodles for a few minutes to moisturize them.

- Once you have obtained the desired consistency for the noodles, drain them and soak them in cold water to stop cooking. Then, book them.

- Continue to heat the pan with a drizzle of oil. Heat it on high heat and then sauté the carrot strips for two minutes.

- Then add the onion and garlic and sauté the whole for another two minutes.

- Then add the pepper strips and, right away, the meat strips. Continue to sauté the ingredients for another 2 or 3 minutes.

- When the meat and vegetables are well cooked, add the noodles and mix everything well, stirring again over high heat.

- Finally, add the soy sauce, remix everything and turn off the heat.

- When serving, sprinkle with chopped parsley leaves.

DINNER

PORTUGUESE COD ACCRAS

Ingredients

- Crumbled and desalinated cod: 8 oz.

- One onion: 2 oz.

- Two cloves of garlic: 0.6 oz.

- Wheat flour: 5 oz.

- Butter: 5 oz.

- Milk: 8 cups

- Olive oil: 1 cup

- Black pepper: As required

- A pinch of nutmeg

- Fresh parsley: 0.5 oz.

- Three eggs: 9 oz.

- Breadcrumbs: 2 oz.

Preparation

- To start, peel and finely cut the onion and garlic. In the case of parsley, wash the leaves well, drain and chisel.

- Heat a drizzle of oil in a non-stick pan over low heat. Once the oil is hot, fry the onion and garlic for a few minutes until the onion becomes transparent.

- Then add the cod meat (drained and dried) and mix everything well. Wait two minutes, remove the mixture from the heat and reserve it in a container.

- Then, we will prepare the béchamel sauce.

- In the same pan you used, heat the butter over low heat until it melts. Then pour the flour and mix it with butter, using a spatula or kitchen spoon.

- Continue to mix the two ingredients until you get a paste. Then, cook it over medium heat, for 1 or 2 minutes, without stopping to stir.

- To continue, stir in a bit of milk and stir until you get a homogeneous mixture. Continue to mix the milk, little by little, until you finish getting a cream. Be sure to remove all lumps. Usually, this procedure will take 10 to 12 minutes. Finally, add the salt and pepper to improve the taste.

- Continue cooking over medium heat for about 5 minutes without stopping to stir the sauce.

- Then add the chopped parsley and the cod and onion mixture. Stir everything until you get a homogeneous and thick paste. You will see that this paste will easily detach from the pan at some point. This consistency will mark the right time to stop the fire.

- Then grease a bowl with a little butter and flour. Then place the preparation inside and cover it with plastic film. If you have a refrigerator, then put it for a minimum of four hours to become stronger and easier to handle.

- After this time, retake the dough and form balls. You can help yourself with two spoons to give shape to the accras. You can decide between a round or rather elongated shape.

- Cover a dish with a mixture of flour and breadcrumbs. Place next to a bowl with the contents of the three eggs, well beaten. Take each dumpling, soak in the beaten eggs, and then cover it with breadcrumbs and flour. Place the accras on a plate and let them air dry, or place them in the refrigerator for some time, so that they dry and harden a little.

- Then, heat a pan over medium heat with oil.

- Once the accras are golden, remove them from the pan and place them in a covered dish. This is to remove the excess oil.

- That's it. Your Portuguese cod accras are ready. Serve immediately and enjoy them hot.

CHAPTER FOURTEEN

DAY TWENTY-ONE: SUCCESSFUL DIETING

Becoming successful in your diet is not much of a big deal anymore for you after following this twenty-one-day diet plan. You will be able to control the amount of food consumed daily and know the nutritional benefit as well. Most significantly, we emphasize natural foods and advise individuals to reduce their consumption of processed foods, trans fats, added sugar, and refined carbohydrates.

WHITE FISH CEVICHE RECIPE

Ingredients

- Sea bream: 3 oz.

- Peruvian or West Indian yellow pepper: 2 oz.

- One large lemon: 5 oz.

- One medium purple onion: 2 oz.

- Three sprigs of fresh coriander: 2 oz.

- Salt: As required

- 1 cup of cooked corn kernels

- One sweet potato

- Potato or plantain corn chips: 3 oz.

Preparation

- First, peel the sweet potato and cook it in a saucepan with boiling water and a pinch of salt. Next, this vegetable must be mashed until it becomes tender, easy to pierce with the tip of a fork.

- Then peel the purple onion and cut it into thin strips. Then, immerse the strips in a container with cool water for 10 minutes. In this way, you will soften the taste of this vegetable a little.

207

- Then wash the chili and cut it into thin strips. Make sure to remove the seeds and the white part of the vegetable flesh. Do this to soften the hot taste of the chili.

- Then clean the fish thoroughly. There should not be any thorns, skin, or other hard parts. Next, cut the flesh of the fish.

- To continue, wash and drain the cilantro. Then, snip the leaves and set them aside.

- Combine the fish, onion, cilantro, and a pinch of salt in a bowl. You can put lemon juice and mix everything well.

- After mixing the ceviche, do not wait more than 10 minutes to serve it. This could cause the fish to overcook, ruining the freshness of your dish.

- Serve your ceviche on a plate or in verrines, accompanied by slices of sweet potato

LUNCH

EGGPLANT SALAD

Ingredients

- One large eggplant: 4 oz.

- ½ cup of purple onion

- Two tomatoes: 3 oz.

- Fresh parsley: 2 oz.

- One lemon: 3 oz.

- Extra virgin olive oil: 1 cup

- Salt: As required

- Pepper: As required

- Olives: 2 oz.

Preparation

- Preheat the oven to 180-200 degrees.

- Chop the eggplant into thick slices.

- Let them marinate for about 10 minutes in a little saltwater to chase away the bitter taste.

- Remove the slices from the water. They should be dried a little and put in the oven, wrapped in aluminum foil. Cook the eggplants for 20 minutes.

- Meanwhile, chop the tomato and onion into small cubes and set them aside. Also, chop a few parsley leaves to taste.

- Ensure that the eggplant cools down.

- Then mix it with the purple onion, tomato, and parsley. Add salt, pepper, lemon, and olive oil to taste. If you want, you can add olives.

BAKED SARDINES

Ingredients

- Fresh sardine fillets: 20 oz.

- ½ cup of onion

- Two cloves garlic: 1 oz.

- Parsley leaves: 1 oz.

- Olive oil: 2 cups

- Salt and black pepper: As required

Preparation

- Clean the sardines. Be careful not to leave any scales or excess thorns.

- Chop the onion, garlic, and parsley into tiny cubes.

- Cover the sardines with onion, garlic, and parsley. Next, you need to add salt, pepper, and add the olive oil.

- Let your sardines marinate for an hour in a covered container.

- Then preheat the oven to 150 ° C.

- In a tray, place all the sardines skin-side down.

- Place the container in the oven for 15 minutes. Remember that sometimes ovens have higher or lower temperatures than stated. So, you should be careful not to burn your sardines or miss cooking.

- Remove the sardines from the oven. You will then turn them over and cook them again for another 5 minutes.

- Take them out of the oven and serve them.

- You can add a little more olive oil when eating.

Following a gastroparesis-friendly diet won't address the disorder's underlying cause but may significantly alleviate day-to-day symptoms. This is correct, especially for people with mild to moderate gastroparesis. Therefore, the standard recommendations are based on the basic science of digestion and the experience and observations of patients and clinicians over time. Here are a few tips to note:

Eat Quietly

Constantly eat in an environment that is as quiet and comfortable as possible. For example, sitting at the table and always setting the table. Avoid distractions with electronic devices (TV, PC, video games, Tablet, or smartphone) during the meal.

Constantly Chew for an Extended Period

This is because the digestion phase in the mouth is of crucial significance. Also, drink water slowly during meals, in moderate amounts; one or two glasses of water are adequate for the meal.

Eat Properly

Fed at breakfast like a prince (meal not plentiful in quantity but rich in nutrients and energy), at lunch like a bourgeois (more abundant and always balanced meal), at dinner like a beggar (meal based mostly on vegetables with whole grains and legumes to have a low energy density).

Eat Completely

Each meal must be complete and must consist of a base of foods rich in carbohydrates, accompanied by proteins, little fats, vitamins, and minerals.

Eat Natural Food

Eat natural foods as much as possible or with a few fries. Avoid canned foods and foods with preservatives.

Made in United States
Troutdale, OR
02/24/2024